DRIVE WITHOUT FEAR

THE INSECURE DRIVER'S GUIDE
TO INDEPENDENCE

DRIVE WITHOUT FEAR

THE INSECURE DRIVER'S GUIDE
TO INDEPENDENCE

By

Norman Klein

ISBN: 1-58721-500-4

This book is printed on acid free paper.

Cartoons are Courtesy Nationwide Insurance Companies,
Columbus, Ohio.

1st Books rev. 5/1/01

About the Book

Drive Without Fear is the culmination of thirty-six years of helping insecure people overcome their fear of driving. It demonstrates conclusively that fear and anxiety will not prevent them from driving if they are strongly motivated. A major portion of the book revolves around true stories of twenty phobic drivers who dramatically overcame their irrational fear of driving. The book also contains innovative solutions to the complex traffic problems which confront frustrated motorists.

The chapter *Steering, The Key to Driving* imparts a unique method for precise steering which demonstrates to readers how to drive safely through the tightest spaces. *Tips for the Elderly* and the chapter *Most Frequent Mistakes Made By New Drivers* will enlighten and ease the angst suffered by phobic drivers.

The chapter on *Accident Free Driving* clearly shows how to avoid situations that could lead to accidents.

An entire chapter is devoted to the intricacies of manual transmission vehicles. A simple driving test is included for those who are unsure of their ability to drive.

Drive Without Fear encompasses nearly every conceivable aspect of driving for today's motorist. Among them:

- A step by step procedure for beginners learning to drive.
- How to use anti lock brakes.
- Driving safely on expressways.
- How to co-exist with trucks on the highway.
- Unique methods for driving on snow.

Digesting the information contained in ***Drive Without Fear*** can dispel the tension and trepidation endured by phobic drivers. Reading this book is like having a good friend alongside you to ease the trauma, a coach who will persevere with you until you succeed.

Drive Without Fear shares the expertise of the author and overcomes the complex social problems that prevent many people from driving. It demonstrates emphatically that the fear of driving can be swept away by utilizing the tested methods of the author.

After reading this book, people with a fear of driving will be encouraged by the successes of the people portrayed. ***Drive Without Fear*** is an important book, which has the power to both change and save peoples' lives.

For my two super sons, Howard and David and in memory of my irreplaceable friend, Martin (Maish) Borowsky

TABLE OF CONTENTS

PREFACE

The original idea of this book was aimed towards women over fifty years of age since they comprised a large number of my students. However, upon reflection, I realized that the knowledge contained in this book can benefit everyone. I have encountered men, as well as young people, who were afraid to drive. Fear has no age limit. Still, there are more elderly women who needed to learn to drive, since many of them depended on their husbands. Unfortunately for them, their husbands either passed away or became incapacitated and unable to drive.

I would like to thank the following individuals without whom this book would not have been written and ultimately, published: Sylvia Magerman for her help in putting together the original manuscript; My dear wife, Marylin; My two sons, David and Howard for their help and encouragement; & Martin Stanger for his technical advice.

Almost everything I learned about teaching driving was derived from the people I taught. I listened to their fears and problems and tried to develop ways to help them. In my career, I helped approximately five thousand people. Hopefully this book will help many thousands more.

INTRODUCTION

There are people who would give almost anything to drive an automobile. They are desperate, but procrastinate. They think they are too nervous. Perhaps they have tried before, but have become discouraged.

Now driving has become a necessity. They are alone and despondent. Without realizing it, they have become completely dependent on other people. Most of the time they stay at home and become depressed with very little to do except watch television.

It could be a middle-aged woman with an incapacitated husband who has become a prisoner in her home because she cannot drive. She may have obtained a driver's license a long time ago, but has not driven for so long that she is afraid to try. Perhaps she is a lonely spinster now retired who finds inactivity unbearable. Driving an automobile could certainly improve her life style.

Books about driving do very little for these people. These books usually concentrate on safe driving habits and rules and regulations of the road. The books assume that the reader has no fear of driving and already knows the basic rudiments (steering, turning, etc.).

What about the nervous learner or the older person whose coordination has diminished? Older people who have never attempted to drive almost always experience difficulty learning to steer. Some driving instructors do not have enough experience and expertise to cope with middle-aged beginners. In many instances, the learner will stop taking lessons, thinking he or she simply cannot learn.

The methodology of teaching older people or anyone with poor coordination differs from those with good motor skills. Ordinary teaching methods are inadequate and infinite patience is a necessity. However, fear of driving is not confined to older women. There are many younger people who have an irrational fear of driving because of some incident which happened when they were very young. Parents with an unnatural fear of driving can pass it onto their children. I have known fearless men who blanched at the thought of driving.

I taught a young man to drive who told me that when he was a child, he was petrified at the thought of going into a restaurant. His family had come here from Europe. His father had never gone into a restaurant. He always spoke of it disparagingly. His children thought a restaurant was an evil place. It took them years before they realized it was merely a place to dine. This is an example of how irrational fears and phobias begin.

When a man is young, it is important for him to drive for social or business reasons. If a man does not drive by the age of thirty, he is probably afraid. Most men who do not drive have a deep seated fear of driving, although they will usually not admit it.

More women than men are afraid to drive. When a woman gets married, her husband takes over the driving. A couple with an average income cannot afford two cars. The husband does not want her to drive. He wants her to stay home, cook and watch the children. He wants to know where she is.

Now when he is older and wiser he realizes his mistake. Perhaps his eyesight is failing. He may have had a stroke or a heart attack. It is not easy for these women. They have been brainwashed for years into believing that they were too nervous or too frightened to drive.

I know from experience that nervousness does not prevent people from learning. Nervousness is not all bad. Nervous drivers tend to be more careful. As they improve, their confidence grows and anxiety gradually diminishes.

Many men and women in their late sixties and early seventies are alert and active. There is no reason why they can not learn to drive. It may take longer than younger people, but it can be done. In my experience only a very small percentage of these women (or men) couldn't learn. These unfortunate people had such poor "motor skills" that they couldn't learn to steer the car precisely.

I devised a simple test for people having difficulty learning to steer. This test proves beyond a doubt whether or not the person in question can learn to steer. Surprisingly, only a small percentage couldn't pass this test. I also have developed easier methods for turning corners safely. This is explained in another chapter.

Fifteen years ago, I wrote a correspondence course for people who wanted to become professional driving instructors. This course was approved and licensed by the Pennsylvania Department of Public Instruction. A few years later I realized how much more important it was for me to convey my methods in a book aimed towards older women and men. I am reasonably certain that the problems I encountered teaching difficult students is a microcosm of what exists in other regions where the automobile is the major form of transportation. Aside from the many people who have never driven before, there are many who have a valid driver's license but are afraid to drive.

I have deliberately repeated and simplified many of the instructions contained in this book. My experience with older students has enabled me to identify with them. I have seen their mistakes and have tried to be as explicit as possible.

Before the automatic transmission with power steering and power brakes was introduced, women drivers were a novelty. That change in automobiles gave women the impetus they needed. Yet today many faint-hearted women (and men) are still reluctant to drive. I hope that reading this book will encourage many of them to reconsider and try to learn how to drive. Most people who learn to drive at a later age learn on a vehicle with automatic transmission. This book deals mainly with this type of automobile. However, a chapter is devoted to stick shift driving.

Some of the women and men I have taught to drive have encouraged me to write this book. I hope this book will encourage and inspire many others to reap the benefit of the various concepts I have developed in the past thirty years. The men and women who overcame their fear are now driving by utilizing the methods in this book. Follow it faithfully and you too will drive.

CHAPTER 1
TRUE EXAMPLES OF PEOPLE WHO SUCCEEDED

Overcoming your fear of driving is not the impossible dream. It is yours for the taking. The phobic drivers described in this book are *real*. They learned to drive despite their irrational fears. Some were propelled by sheer desperation. Others simply refused to succumb to these fears and ultimately learned to drive.

Contrary to what you may believe, nervousness will not prevent you from learning to drive an automobile. I have seen it happen hundreds of times. Your fear of driving will subside and your confidence will grow as you improve. Many men and women are disheartened by news reports concerning people getting killed or crippled in automobile accidents. A large percentage of these accidents are caused by intoxicated drivers or by others who drive recklessly, carelessly and thoughtlessly.

Many of my students have confided in me and related how for years they were afraid to drive. They would conjure visions of themselves behind the wheel having accidents. Positive imaging is extremely important. People behave outwardly in the manner they imagine they will behave. Negative thoughts about driving could prevent them from trying to learn. Picture yourself driving an automobile smoothly and confidently. Do not imagine yourself pushing the accelerator instead of the brake or crashing off a cliff. Too many older men and women are convinced that they cannot learn to drive.

If driving was that difficult, how could many millions of people all over the world be driving? Take one step at a time. You don't have to drive on expressways or turnpikes! You can be very happy being a neighborhood driver. A certain doctor in Philadelphia advised all of his recently widowed patients to learn how to drive. Some who took his advice eventually were able to stop taking tranquilizers. Almost anyone who can learn to steer an automobile can learn to drive. When I started to teach people how to drive, I observed the difficulty older people encountered learning to steer. In time, I developed methods and procedures which proved successful in almost every instance.

Before you enter the driving arena, it would be helpful to have some knowledge of the traffic problems you will encounter. It is not easy for an inexperienced older driver to apply "common sense" when confronted with different situations. "Common sense" can't be applied unless the subject is understood, especially for older people unfamiliar with the many diverse traffic regulations. Driving an automobile in today's traffic has become more complicated than it was years ago.

Surprisingly, only a small percentage of the people who came to me for driving lessons could not learn to steer the automobile. This included students up to the age of seventy-two. Young people learn to steer much sooner than older people but, occasionally, even a teenager who does not have good "motor skills" will have problems. The small percentage of students who did not learn, either had extremely poor "motor skills" or they did not have the patience and determination to continue.

Of all the people I have taught to drive, Betty V. epitomizes the importance of determination and perseverance. Betty depended on her husband for everything. He passed away when she was sixty-seven years old. She was devastated and depressed. Betty didn't know a brake pedal from an accelerator.

Betty was obsessed with the fear that someday, she would be like the little white haired old ladies who clutched each other as they walked across the street. She was not a good candidate for driving. Her "motor skills" were not good. She was extremely frightened. At first she did not listen to my instructions. At one point I suggested that she forget about driving. However, she was adamant. In the midst of many tears, trials and errors, she declared she would never stop trying.

Betty couldn't seem to concentrate on what I wanted her to do. No one I taught tried my patience as she did. She couldn't seem to remember to keep her foot on the brake when changing from "R" to "D" or from "D" to "R". I spent hours with her going forward ten feet and back ten feet until she remembered to hold her foot on the brake when changing gears. She mastered this because she persevered and would not stop trying to learn to drive. She may have been the slowest student I ever taught, but I admired her for her tenacity. Many women with more ability than Betty are not driving today because they did not have her determination.

There were a few I stopped trying to teach almost immediately because I considered them unteachable. I considered Betty to be marginal. When she stopped crying she did show slight signs of improvement.

Because she was so insistent, I stayed with her for two years. The bottom line is she bought a car and is now driving in her neighborhood. Betty will never be a complete driver, but she takes her ailing mother to the doctor and she can do her shopping without imposing on others. I saw her recently and she happily informed me that after four years of driving, she has never had an accident. She has also stopped crying. She is no longer concerned about crossing streets in her old age while holding onto another older woman.

Dorothy was seventy years old when her husband died. She had tried to drive when she was a young woman, but had stopped trying because her husband did not encourage her. She was completely alone in the world. Dorothy's "motor skills" were excellent for her age. Her only problem was a deep rooted fear of driving. She did so well after six hours of instruction that her fear began to diminish. She passed the driving test on her first attempt after ten driving lessons. She asked me to take her out in her car a few times. Her husband always liked a big car so she was a little hesitant about driving it. With encouraging words from me, she had no difficulty driving her car. I advised her to stay in her neighborhood for a few months before venturing out further. I met her in a food store two years later. Dorothy was exuberant. She told me she drove everywhere. Driving a car kept her occupied and was good therapy for her loneliness.

There are probably millions of lonely women who could be driving if they would only try. Do not become discouraged if you have a steering problem. No matter how poorly you drive in the beginning, you can learn if you continue to show the slightest improvement. I know it can be done. I have taught many who seemed hopeless in the beginning.

Lil thought she was hopeless. She was in a desperate situation. Her husband was a "manic depressive" and his condition was deteriorating. She worked in a hospital a half mile from her home. She no longer could depend on her husband to drive her to work. She was fifty-four years old and four feet, eight inches tall. An upholsterer made a special cushion to enable her to sit comfortably because she was so tiny.

Lil decided to go to a large driving school for lessons. It was a disaster. She was shuttled back and forth among four different instructors. None of them knew how to cope with her. One of them told her she would never drive.

Lil was distraught, but didn't want to stop trying. A woman in the hospital suggested calling me. I started to give her driving lessons and although she was very nervous and hesitant at the beginning, I assured her that she could learn. Lil was no worse than the hundreds of women I had taught to drive. I discovered that when she made right and left turns, she pushed the accelerator too much. As a result, she could not straighten out in time. This is not unusual for middle aged beginners or any new driver.

I advised her not to touch the accelerator when turning from a stopped position and to let the automobile glide with no pressure on the accelerator. I also told her to look straight ahead after the turn. She was amazed at the results. After a few hours of practice, she mastered the turns. With her confidence restored Lil went on to become on of my best students. Six months after she obtained her driver's license, Lil called me to tell me she drove from Philadelphia to Long Island by herself.

Betty, Dorothy and Lil are not isolated examples. Their very survival depended on whether or not they could drive an automobile. What is needed is persistence, tenacity and determination. Dorothy once tried when she was in her thirties. She tried again in her seventies and was successful.

It is obvious that city driving presents more hazards and complications than small towns or back road driving. However, no matter where you drive, the basics are the same. Before driving on your own, you must master steering the car precisely, executing left and right turns correctly, and being able to go back in reverse accurately.

Those of you who already have a driver's license are fortunate since you do not have to take a driving test. If you do not have a license, don't despair. I have taught hundreds of middle-aged women and men who have succeeded in passing the state examination.

I do not recommend anyone over sixty years of age to learn on a stick shift car. If you must drive this type of car, it is extremely important to first learn on a car with automatic transmission. Take the driving examination in the car with automatic transmission. After you pass the test, you can learn on a stick shift car. I have included a chapter on driving this type of automobile. However, I strongly urge anyone over sixty to drive an automatic transmission car with power steering and power brakes.

No matter how frightened people are about driving, they will learn if strongly motivated. In most instances, nervousness will not stop a person from learning. Extremely poor "motor skills" can prevent people from learning how to drive. Most people do not have poor "motor skills". Nervousness disappears gradually as your skill and confidence grows. The more you practice, the less nervous you become. Motor skills can be improved.

Many older women would love to drive, but they lack the determination, courage and patience to follow through to success. They make a half hearted attempt to learn and at the slightest setback resign themselves that driving is not for them. They talk about it constantly becoming increasingly boring to anyone who will listen. Some of these women have friends or relatives who take them shopping, to doctors, beauty parlors, etc. How long can these women impose on others. Circumstances and situations are constantly changing. Perhaps two or three years from now these same women will not be the beneficiary of charitable friends and relatives.

It is true that most young people learn to drive an automobile quickly. A twelve year old boy or girl can probably learn how to drive a car quicker than any other age group. However, anyone that age would be too immature to drive safely. Some women stop trying to learn because they are having difficulty steering the automobile. These women must realize that they will not learn quickly. They should not look for reasons to quit, but instead realize how important it is for them to continue.

A slow learner does not suddenly learn to drive. Learning is a gradual process. You must have patience and realize that once you learn how to steer the auto, stay in the lane and turn corners properly, you will go on to become a capable driver. Many of my slower students have become better drivers than some who learned quickly.

For many a widow the challenge of learning to drive can help her through a trying period. By staying busy, she can ease the pain of her loss. The therapeutic value of learning to drive is immeasurable for a grieving widow. Marge was afraid to drive alone. She knew how to drive and had been driving for twelve years. After fifteen years of marriage, her husband died of cancer. She stayed at his side until he passed away. Five years later she remarried. For seven years she was happy with her new husband.

Unfortunately, one morning, without any warning, her husband suffered a massive heart attack and died almost instantly. This second tragedy in her life had a traumatic effect on her. Her few relatives lived in another city. For months she hardly went out of her apartment. Marge lost her desire to mingle with other people.

Marge had an automobile, but when she decided to drive for the first time since her husband's death, she froze at the wheel. She got out of the car almost in a state of shock. She could feel her heart pounding.

A month later she decided to call a driving school. Marge took six one-hour lessons but her driving was tentative. She stopped taking lessons. In spite of her need for driving her car, she seemed powerless. She would get behind the wheel but could not muster enough courage to move the car. It appeared that the shock of witnessing the demise of her two husbands had made her agoraphobic. For some unknown reason agoraphobia affects women more than men. It is a mental sickness that is sometimes caused by the loss of a loved one. Many women afflicted with this condition are afraid to leave their homes and reluctant to mingle with other people. Recent experiments have proven that agoraphobic people can overcome their problems by doing what they feared in spite of pounding heart beats and sweaty palms.

Marge called me and told me about her problem. I proceeded to give her driving lessons. As long as I sat beside her, she drove beautifully. I tried to convince her to drive alone, but she told me she was not ready. After listening to her excuses for a few weeks, I devised a plan to help her.

She lived in a suburban apartment building which was away from city traffic. The building was surrounded by a quiet circular rural area leading back to the building. Without telling her what I had in mind, I arrived one day wearing my jogging shoes. After driving around the building a few times, I told her what I wanted to do.

My plan was simple. I would jog along her side as she drove slowly. At first she protested, but I finally convinced her to try. As she drove slowly, I jogged near the car and talked to her as if I was sitting beside her. Occasionally, she panicked, and I stopped. After a few minutes, she started out again with me jogging along with words of encouragement.

The next three times I saw her I continued with the same procedure. Each time she showed improvement and appeared more confident. Now I felt she was ready for the next step. Instead of jogging, I stood outside the car and asked her to drive around the building while I waited for her. After much coaxing, she drove slowly around the building to where I was waiting. We repeated this on her next two lessons.

I wanted her to drive by herself into the city streets, but she said she was not ready. I told her that if her progress was halted, she would regress into her previous fear of driving alone. We decided that I would drive first and she would follow me in her car. The first time I drove about one mile while she followed me. I drove slowly and if she got too far behind, I waited for her.

When we returned, she was elated. We went out four more times. Each time I went a little further.

Finally I persuaded her to go out alone. Marge drove around the block carefully. After she came back, she surprised me. She drove off and went to the market place which was a few miles away. When Marge returned, she announced that no matter how frightened she was, she would continue to drive alone until her fear was obliterated. Marge finally drove despite her fear because her desire and determination to drive was stronger than her fear.

Helen K. and Jean R. had similar problems. Both were in their early seventies. Both had ailing husbands and both of them wanted to drive.

Helen's husband had lost most of his eyesight, and Jean's husband had Parkinson's disease. Jean and Helen each had a driver's license which they had obtained when they were young. Neither one knew how to drive very well.

Helen took her driving lessons faithfully until she was able to drive her husband to his doctor and to the supermarket, etc. Jean made excuses and canceled her lessons. They both had equal ability. Helen was determined to learn no matter how long it took. Jean did not have the courage and foresight to continue. Now she sits in her apartment with her sick husband watching him deteriorate, and she has to depend on others for transportation.

There are thousands of women like Jean who must depend on others for help. It doesn't have to be that way. Jean wanted to drive as much as Helen. Her ability was equal to Helen's. Her need was as great as Helen's. Yet she could not conquer her fear. She lacked the will and courage to continue. In my experience, I have come across some women who had good "motor skills" but they never completed their driver training. These women wanted to drive and needed to drive. Yet some characteristic in their personality made them vacillate, and procrastinate until they succumbed to their inner fear.

These women wanted to drive for the same reasons. Almost for survival. Yet they failed. Could part of the answer be in their genes? Twenty years ago I taught a young physician how to drive. He had poor motor skills. He needed many driving lessons before he learned to drive. He was a brilliant scientist, but his coordination was not too good. Afterwards, I taught his teenage son and daughter and guess what? The two of them had difficulty learning. They suffered from the same characteristics as their father. Poor motor skills.

I wonder if we as humans are limited in what we can achieve because of inherited characteristics from our family ancestors? Even this could be overcome by fierce determination.

Many people do not realize the potential within themselves. Lack of confidence and fear of failure prevent them from reaching their objective. How often a person with a handicap will excel more than others with more natural ability. A person's inner drive cannot be measured. Champions invariably have a deep desire to excel in whatever activity they are involved in. A good example is Pete Rose. He never had a great throwing arm nor could he run very fast. Yet because of his fierce competitiveness and his desire to be the best, he has set records that may stand for many years.

It does not matter how timid or frightened you are about driving. Don't surrender to your fear. Keep trying and you will learn to drive. One of the reasons why many people are afraid to drive is that they cannot picture themselves able to drive through tight spaces. When they are in a car as a passenger, they cringe as cars pass them both coming toward them or cars passing from behind.

Once new drivers learn to use their eyes correctly and not stare at distractions, they will master steering the car. With enough practice, and concentration the fear of driving through narrow spaces will disappear. Some of you may think you will never overcome the fear of narrow spaces, but if you persist, you will be amazed at the positive results. If you are in good health physically and mentally you should be able to drive a car regardless of your age. However, if you once drove a long time ago, driving will be easier than if you never drove before.

At age seventy-five, Elizabeth had no intention of ever driving an automobile. When she was in her early twenties (fifty years ago) she learned how to drive, but did no driving after she obtained her driver's license. Elizabeth never married. While working in Sears, she became acquainted with Margaret. They became life-long friends. When they retired they decided to move into a retirement home. Margaret always had a car so there never was a transportation problem.

Not feeling well, Margaret went to her doctor. After the examination she received disastrous news. Margaret was terminally ill with bone cancer. As time went by, she was hospitalized. She told Elizabeth to take care of her car. Elizabeth had no alternative. She decided to try to learn to drive.

At age seventy-five she was alert and physically sound. I gave her ten driving lessons on my driver training car and then proceeded to teach her on the car she received from Margaret. Elizabeth only wanted to drive to the supermarket, her dentist, doctor, etc. She accomplished her goal and now doesn't have to ask anyone for transportation.

She is actually chauffeuring other retirees to the supermarket. It's amazing what new drivers can accomplish if they do not quit at the slightest setback. Think of the reward. No more asking people for favors. You will be independent and free to go anywhere you choose. Those who are extremely nervous about driving will be frightened and apprehensive in the beginning. I have witnessed this with many women and men. Almost like magic these symptoms subside for those who persevere. I have seen the most frightened women (and men) gradually lose their fear and become competent drivers. Remember that you will not have the fear later on that you have in the beginning. As you improve, your anxiety will gradually diminish. Many find this difficult to believe. I have seen this happen hundreds of times. Be fair to yourself. Don't surrender.

CHAPTER 2
MORE ABOUT PEOPLE WHO OVERCAME THE FEAR OF DRIVING

You have a driver's license, but you were never an experienced driver. You have not driven for twenty years. You finally decide to try again. You get behind the wheel with an instructor, your husband or friend. Your palms are sweaty, your hands are trembling. As you start driving, you are thinking, "I'll never drive. I'm just too scared. Why am I torturing myself?"

I have been with new drivers many times with these thoughts. If this happens to you, you must realize that your irrational fear of driving is temporary. You will not be as frightened if you continue to drive. Your fear will diminish, your palms will not sweat and you might even hum a song. Don't quit. I promise you that you will conquer your fear.

If you are extremely nervous the first time, don't try to do too much. Drive a short distance with your companion. Start out in a quiet area. Know exactly where you will go before you start out. Do not drive for more than thirty minutes.

Some people tell new drivers to go right out into heavy traffic. Nothing could be worse for a timid driver. Going into busy streets too soon could frighten a new driver so much, she or he might never drive again. Therefore, it is advisable to gradually increase your driving radius as your ability and confidence grows. A neophyte driver would probably stop driving at the slightest negative incident or accident.

Unfortunately, people have different hangups or phobias. Many people are afraid to speak before a large audience. Some of the most effective speakers will tell you that they were not always comfortable speaking to a large group. They succeeded only because they persevered until they conquered their fear. Perhaps some of them were afraid of being laughed at. Others were nervous just thinking about it. Many times, I have watched a well known personality on television commit a "faux pax" while speaking. He joked about his mistakes and the audience smiled with him. A phobia is defined as an unreasonable fear. Every phobia can be overcome by determination and tenacity.

Believe it or not, your fear of driving will diminish in spite of yourself. It happens in spite of your fear. Your driving will improve as long as you continue. How do I know this? I have witnessed this turnabout many times.

Jack was a typical example. He originally lived in New York. His parents were petrified about driving. As a child, he heard them speaking constantly about their fear of driving. Naturally this adverse atmosphere affected him so that he was too frightened to try to drive. He became fascinated with a form of therapy known as Shiatsu. He told me that it was comparable to acupuncture without the puncture part. He referred to it as acupressure. He took a course in Shiatsu at a New York school and proceeded to practice it. People came to him with muscular problems, arthritis, etc. Some of his patients could not travel so he had to go to them. He wasted too much time traveling on trains and buses. Up to this time, he had been taking half-hearted driving lessons every two or three weeks. When I told him that I was thinking of retiring soon, he decided to take the plunge.

In the beginning, his fear was very obvious. He worried about everything on the street whether it was moving or stationary. When another vehicle passed us or turned around the corner on the other side of us, he wanted to turn the wheel abruptly. He would want to stop at intersections for no logical reason except that he was afraid.

In spite of his fear, he started to improve. His confidence grew after ten hours of driving. Now that his initial fear was subsiding, his improvement became more rapid.

What happened to Jack, happens to almost everyone who perseveres. Now he was able to talk to me on any subject while driving and yet react properly to the traffic scene. He admitted to me that although he was still afraid, he could cope with the challenge of driving. He passed the driving examination on his first attempt and went on to buy an automobile. Now he is able to see more patients, save time, and improve his business.

Some learners are afraid to drive in the rain while others are afraid to drive at night. Some people I have taught were only able to take their lessons at night. They became so accustomed to driving at night that they preferred driving at night more than driving during the day.

I am not suggesting that you should try to drive during a heavy rain, but do not be afraid of driving during a light rain. Once you get over your fear, you will be more relaxed. When you stop, touch the brake gingerly. If your tires are good, you will have no problems.

Without the will to drive, you cannot succeed. Half hearted attempts will fail. Mildred G. had a valid driver's license but had not driven for thirty years. She was convinced that she would never drive. She had two married children who had to shop for her and take her to doctors, etc. Her husband had passed away. She was sixty-two years old which was certainly not too old, especially since she did not have to take a driver's test.

Mildred's children had problems of their own and pressured her into calling me. Mildred finally called me just to quiet her children. She had no intention of learning how to drive. After taking two lessons, she told me she couldn't continue. Her attempt at driving was half hearted. She told her children she tried, but she couldn't do it. She didn't want to drive, but wanted to satisfy them that she tried. She will never be independent and will have to rely on others for the rest of her life. She was completely lacking in courage. If you want to drive, you cannot be a quitter. Those who are strongly motivated will conquer their fear.

At the age of sixty-two Mrs. Meyers had a problem. Her husband had become disabled. He could no longer drive. They had no relatives. He had to work since he was not old enough to receive Social Security and he needed a few more years to get a pension from his job. All she had to do was drive him a half a mile to the train so he could go to work.

She needed many lessons. Her motor skill was not great. She persevered and finally passed the driver's test. She drove to the train stop at least twenty times with me. I sat in the car a few times while she drove her husband to the train stop. She told me she was ready to take him without me. However, that was not the end of the story. Ten years later, I walked into a bakery to buy bread. The lady who waited on me stared at me and smiled. She was an older woman whose hair was dyed dark red. "Don't you know me," she said. I looked at her closely and recognized her. It was Mrs. Meyers. She told me that her husband had passed away two years ago. The bakery store was three miles from her house. She said that if she couldn't drive, she would not have been able to get the job and learning to drive was her salvation.

Rose and Cy were very compatible. So much so that they were both afraid to drive. Rose was a new driver. Cy had been driving for thirty years. Somewhere along the way Cy became agoraphobic about driving far from his home. He was afraid of driving over bridges, afraid of driving on multi-lane highways and afraid of driving to new places. Cy was an experienced driver, but he developed an irrational fear of driving. Rose had passed the driving test thirty years previously, but her husband's fear affected her. Time went by and she stopped driving. Now, the problem.

They had a married son who lived in a town about thirty miles from them. When their son and his wife had a baby, Rose and Cy could not see their grandchild unless their son visited them. Cy went to a psychiatrist four times, but to no avail. I tried to encourage him to drive with me, but he refused. I decided to forget about him temporarily and concentrate on Rose. The way to the son's house was not complicated. Only three turns were involved. However, on the way was a multi-lane highway which only lasted for fifteen minutes. This highway was not too busy if you went after the morning rush hour.

I told Rose that I would take her in her automobile. Cy said he would come along and perhaps try to drive on the way back. On the morning we were supposed to go, Cy said he changed his mind. He had spent a sleepless night and could not go. I didn't try to persuade him and Rose and I went without him. Rose was apprehensive, but she realized that if Cy wouldn't do it, then it was up to her. We completed the entire trip without any problem. The traffic was light. Rose did very well. As she drove, she became more relaxed. She knew now that she would eventually be able to drive to her son's house.

The following week we went again. This time Cy said he would like to come along. I told him, I did not expect him to drive and Rose would drive both ways. Knowing we did not expect him to drive, Cy did not have a sleepless night. Cy sat in the back seat and Rose proceeded to drive. She drove very well again. On the way back, I assured Cy that we did not want him to drive.

The next time we went, Cy asked if he could drive back. I agreed and he got behind the wheel. Cy was an excellent driver. He had no trouble at all. When we got back, he admitted that he was scared, but he felt that if Rose could do it, so could he. He knew he was much more experienced than Rose and he felt ashamed that he was putting the burden on her. The rest of the story has a happy ending. I went with them one more time and they drive there almost every week. Now they are not strangers to their granddaughter.

I would like to mention some of the people who are driving now despite their handicaps:

1.   A deaf mute in her middle thirties who is now driving.

2.   A girl with polio whom I taught in her car with hand controls.

3.   A man who was so afflicted that he could not stand for more than ten seconds. He drove to work and then got into his wheel chair.

4.   A sailor with one arm.

5.   A woman who trembled constantly because of an accident at her birth.

6.   Four people with vision in one eye.

7.   A girl and young man who had learning disabilities.

8.   A man who only had the use of his right leg.

9.   A boy whose growth was stunted and who had difficulty walking.

These are nine people who wanted to drive desperately in spite of their handicap. They all succeeded. How many of you have no handicap, but are afraid to drive? Your fear of driving exists only in your mind. Unless you are mentally incompetent or are physically unable to drive, you owe it to yourself to try.

People have all kinds of phobias. Most of them are surmountable. In some instances meditation will help you. Your subconscious is dictating to you and telling you that you can't drive. For ten minutes every day, sit down in a comfortable chair in a darkened room. Close your eyes and repeat to yourself, "I can drive." Try to picture yourself driving smoothly. Constant repetition of positive thinking will convince your subconscious that you can drive. Once you are actually driving, you will realize that you can do it. Almost everyone I taught told me after the first lesson that it wasn't as bad as they thought it would be. The fear of driving is comparable to many other illogical fears. Some people are afraid of going into deep water. They never learn how to swim, but almost everyone can learn. Learning how to drive is easier than learning how to type. It takes a year for anyone to become proficient at typing. Driving an auto can be learned in ten to twenty hours. Of course, you won't be an expert, but that will come in due time. All phobias are only in your mind. In reality, they do not exist.

When I am teaching people (not teenagers) who drive too fast and turn corners too fast, I usually know the problem. These learners are afraid of the cars behind them. If they have to execute a right turn, they go too fast especially if an automobile is behind them.

When this happens, I tell the learner to pull over to the side. I inform my nervous beginner not to worry since our right signal is advising all traffic behind us that we are turning right at the intersection. Also by using the brake pedal, the brake lights will go on. The driver behind will either slow down or go around us.

When you are a new driver you are easily recognizable. Considerate drivers will try to pass you without honking the horn. There are some who will be annoyed. Let them.

They were all new drivers at one time. People forget very easily.

Everyone slows down when turning around corners. The smaller the street, the slower you must move. The drivers behind you understand this. If you do not have your car under control, you could have an accident. Stay to the right and other drivers will pass you. For approximately six months you will drive slower than the average driver. You don't have to keep up with traffic. Some people drive with no patience. You must stay at a speed within your control. Don't be intimidated. There are all kinds of people in the world. There are also all kinds of drivers. If you drive faster because you are afraid of the drivers behind you, you are bound to have an accident. You are the one who will suffer. Your insurance rates will increase. You are the one who may get hurt. Don't let impatient drivers affect your driving.

Cartoon A: Danger High Explosives

CHAPTER 3
OVERCOMING THE FEAR OF DRIVING AND AN INTERVIEW WITH A RECOVERED PHOBIC DRIVER

Almost everyone has at least one illogical fear. Here is a list of some of them:

Fear Of heights
Fear of crowds
Fear of getting fat
Fear of lightning
Fear of getting thin
Fear of spiders
Fear of deep water
Fear of mice

Fear of ships
Fear of animals
Fear of flying
Fear of Friday the 13th
Fear of elevators
Fear of dying
Fear of public speaking
Fear of dogs

Every one of these fears is irrational except to the person who has it.

In almost every case, there is no reason for each fear. Most of these fears started when the person was young and impressionable.

I remember teaching a young lady who was terribly frightened by lightning and thunder. Her mother would hide in the closet during a storm. She and her mother became panicky whenever a thunderstorm came along. I once taught a very nervous woman how to drive. She constantly spoke about her fear in front of her eight year old child. The day I took her for her driving test, the child was nauseous and had an upset stomach.

A girl grew up hating men because her father walked out on her family when she was a child. A bitter mother turned her against men. Many people with deep rooted fears need help. Not all of them conquer their fears, but many are able to lead normal lives after years of psychoanalysis.

Sometimes fear can disappear as a person gets older. When I was a child, I stepped into a hole while ocean bathing and almost drowned. For awhile I was afraid of walking in the ocean, but as time went by I realized my fear was unreasonable. Every fear I have mentioned is curable, but many people go through a lifetime suffering from their own particular phobia.

A person who is afraid of high places will try to avoid standing on a high platform or a high building. If you are afraid of talking to a group of people you usually avoid that situation. If you are afraid of going on a ship, you don't go on ships. If you are afraid of flying, you travel by train. There are ways of getting around most fears, but what about driving! Driving an automobile is an integral part of life in every civilized country. It is the most popular form of transportation.

A married woman may have a reasonable excuse for not driving because her husband drives. Of course, she cannot be wholly independent until she drives. A woman who has small children cannot always depend on neighbors to help her. It is hard to believe that in these times there are men who are afraid to drive. In many instances his wife does the driving. Other times neither he or his wife drives. When they have children, they are severely handicapped.

About fifteen years ago, I received a call from a very frightened man. I'll call him Kenny. When he was ten years old, he was in a car accident. From that day on, he was very uneasy sitting in a car. Now in his late twenties, he was soon to be married. His future wife was constantly putting pressure on him to learn how to drive. Kenny decided to seek professional counseling. He had at least ten sessions with a psychiatrist, but he still was afraid to try to drive.

This was the problem as I perceived it. The best way for the doctor to help Kenny was to take him in a car and talk to him while he attempted to drive. Of course, this was preposterous. The psychiatrist was not trained to teach people to drive. Kenny called me and told me the problem. I advised him to continue seeing the doctor and to take driving lessons with me.

Kenny was a good athlete. He had excellent coordination. Good athletes usually learn to drive a car quickly. At first he was jumpy behind the wheel. I had to caution him about pressing the brake too hard. Eventually the combination of the doctor's therapy and driving with me began to take effect. He overcame his fear and became a capable driver. I do not mean to infer that everyone with a fear of driving should see a psychiatrist. In most cases, you can overcome your fear by being strongly motivated.

If you are afraid of being killed in a car accident–don't you sit in a car when someone else is driving! Isn't your physical well being in someone else's hands? Millions of people are driving. However, the quality of your life will certainly be improved if you learn to drive.

The civilized world needs better, safer drivers. There are too many impatient, irresponsible drivers. A person who is afraid at the beginning usually becomes a good driver. He or she will not disregard traffic rules and will not be reckless. The world needs safe drivers so do not procrastinate any longer. **Do it now!!**

INTERVIEW WITH A RECOVERED PHOBIC DRIVER

Question:What made you stop driving?

Answer:One day I had a panic attack while crossing a bridge.

Question:What happened?

Answer:I had become nervous and anxious about driving in unfamiliar places. When I approached the bridge, I thought I was having a heart attack. I somehow managed to cross the bridge. After that incident, my fears increased until I only drove to places with which I was familiar.

Question:Were you afraid of having an accident?

Answer:Not as much as I was afraid of having a stroke or a heart attack.

Question:Did you think you would ever drive on an Interstate highway or over bridges again?

Answer:I knew that somehow I had to conquer my fear or I would lose my independence.

Question:What else was affected by limiting your driving?

Answer:My self esteem suffered. I was also embarrassed when relatives and friends asked me to pick them up at the airport or other places where I was afraid to drive.

Question:What did you do when this first happened?

Answer:I took medication for my nerves, but that did not help.

Question:How did you finally overcome your fear and anxiety about driving?

Answer:I called Norman Klein who was recommended to me as someone who specialized in teaching nervous drivers. While Mr. Klein was in my car, I was able to drive everywhere. We started out slowly and eventually, I drove on busier streets and highways. Finally, we drove over a major bridge which I would never have been able to do on my own. Then, once I became more confident, I followed Mr. Klein's car over the bridge in my car by myself. After that, I knew that I would overcome my fears and eventually, I did.

Question:What finally caused you to do something about your fear of driving?

Answer:Although I was frightened, I knew I had to drive for my survival, especially after my husband suffered a heart attack. I contacted Mr. Klein and I am now an independent person and drive wherever I please.

Question:Do you have a message for nervous phobic drivers?

Answer:Yes. I believe that if you are motivated enough, you can conquer your fear of driving.

"I always straddle the white line, just to be safe."

Cartoon B: I always straddle the white line, just to be safe

CHAPTER 4
STEERING–THE KEY TO DRIVING

For a person just learning to drive, steering is the most important phase of driving. Older people who have never attempted to drive, invariably have problems learning how to steer the car correctly. However, if certain rules are followed almost everyone can learn how to steer an automobile.

RULES TO REMEMBER

1. Never watch the nose of the car.
2. Look straight ahead. Aim high.
3. Do not try to straighten out the front of the car.
4. Do not watch the sides of the car.
5. Do not try to keep the steering wheel straight.
6. Guide your body not the car.

All of these rules are irrevocable. They must be followed implicitly. Let's discuss them one at a time:

Never watch the nose of the car

This is tantamount to watching your nose when you are walking. A bus driver sits up against the window. There is no hood in front of him. This great big bus is behind him. Yet he steers the bus with no problem. How does he follow the road? He simply looks straight ahead.

Look straight ahead

In order to stay in the lane, you must look straight ahead eye level, in the middle of the lane. At a speed of twenty-five miles per hour you look in the center of your lane about a half to one block away. On the open highway at higher speeds, you look straight ahead almost as far as your eyes can see. As you drive, your eyes should be looking up and down the road. This does not mean that you do not move your vision away from the center of your lane. Competent drivers change their vision almost constantly to detect anything moving at the sides. Novices cannot see everything at the beginning but with more experience, they will learn to use their vision more effectively.

Do not try to straighten out the front of the car

This could be the most common mistake learners make. Many new drivers think that while driving, they should try to keep the car straight. Consequently they persist in watching the front of the car. They jiggle the wheel back and forth and are constantly turning the wheel.

Very few streets are perfectly straight. The car should be following the road. If the road is on an angle, the car should be on the same angle. The only way to follow the angle of the road is to look ahead into the center of the lane. This rule is firm. Never watch the front of the car.

Do not watch your fenders

A very common complaint of learners is that they have poor judgment of space on the side. They are afraid of driving through tight spaces. This is especially true of senior citizens. The space around you is not judged by watching the sides of your car. Space is judged best by looking into the center of your lane.

This is a typical situation that may cause the new driver some apprehension. A woman is driving on a street wide enough for her car, parked cars on both sides, and a car coming towards her. If she stares at the car coming towards her, she may turn toward the parked cars. By looking at the oncoming car instead of her lane, she gets the illusion that she is heading directly towards the oncoming car. She must force herself to look straight ahead in the center of the space between the parked cars on her right and the oncoming cars. As she guides her body through that space, the car will move accurately in her lane.

28

Many new drivers have another problem on the same type of street just discussed. When there are no cars coming they tend to drive too close to the parked cars on the right. Hundreds of new drivers have confessed to me their inability to judge the space on the right. The solution is simple. I tell them to drive so their left shoulder is always near the middle of the street. In this manner they will have a few feet of space on the right without encroaching on the other half of the street. When a car comes toward them, they again look in the middle of the space between the parked cars and those coming towards them.

FIG. 1 - DRIVER IS CORRECTLY LOOKING STRAIGHT AHEAD

FIG. 2 DRIVER IS INCORRECTLY LOOKING AT ONCOMING CAR

Parking in Garage

You must not watch the sides of your car when you park in your garage or you will eventually scrape the car. Mark a stripe with paint or chalk in the center of the wall facing you. When you drive into the garage point your body towards the stripe. The car will be centered in the garage and you should have almost equal space on both sides of your car. When backing out of the garage, let the car roll out slowly. Before you go back, make your wheels straight so the car will go out without having to turn the steering wheel. Never run the motor with the garage door closed. The carbon monoxide created can be fatal. Remember that you cannot smell the presence of carbon monoxide.

Turning the wheel too much

Do not turn the wheel hand over hand on a road which requires slight turning or when going on a curve. This will cause the car to oversteer. Simply turn the wheel slightly to the left or right without lifting your hands off the wheel.

It is not a common habit, but some new drivers take their hands off the wheel to make a slight steering correction. They should keep their hands on the wheel to make the necessary correction.

Do not try to keep steering wheel straight

It is not unusual for learners to try to keep the wheel straight while driving. This reminds me of an amusing incident. I was teaching a woman who lived on a narrow winding street with many parked cars. At that time I had a Chevrolet Impala. In the center of the steering wheel on the horn was the engraved figure of an impala. The young woman started the car and proceeded to steer very erratically. I put my hand on the wheel and looked at her. She was staring at the impala on the wheel and frantically trying to keep the figure of the impala straight. This incident is not as far fetched as it seems. Many people are under the same impression as this woman. You must look ahead and guide your body wherever you want to go. The wheel does not have radar and does not have a brain. You, the driver, have a brain and vision.

<u>Guide your body –not the car</u>

This is the key to learning how to steer. You must look precisely where you want to go. If you watch the car, you will drive out of your lane. In order to guide the car, you must look ahead in the center of your lane. If you cannot stay in your lane, you cannot drive. Almost everyone can learn to steer, provided they use their eyes correctly. Instead of trying to guide the nose of the car, you guide your own nose. Your nose together with the correct use of your vision is your compass. Where your nose goes, the car will go. A former student of mine remarked that when she drives, she looks ahead as if she is walking. I can also add to look ahead as if you were riding a bicycle.

I was teaching a sixty-eight year old woman a long time ago. She was having a problem steering. She couldn't seem to take her eyes away from the nose of the car. Finally I told her to stop and spent a few minutes telling her to aim high with her eyes. We continued, but her steering was still erratic. I looked at her. She was looking up at the sky. When I asked her where she was looking she told me that she was looking at the clouds in the sky in front of us.

This is not a fabrication. She actually was looking up at the clouds. Eventually, I convinced her to come down from the clouds and she finally learned how to drive. It wasn't easy, but she was determined since her husband was very ill.

AUTOMATIC TRANSMISSION CARS DO NOT DRIVE WITHOUT GUIDANCE

About fifteen years ago, I was trying to teach a Russian immigrant how to drive. Instead of watching the road, she kept looking at the scenery around her. At the same time, I had to hold my hand on the steering wheel in order to stay on the road. Finally, I said to her, "Olga, you must look in front of you to see where you are going." She turned to me and said with annoyance, "I thought this car was automatic." Laughing, I explained to her that cars do not drive without guidance by the driver.

Steering a shopping cart

Steering an automobile is comparable to steering a shopping cart. When guiding a cart, you would not look as far, but it is just as important to look straight ahead. If you watch the front of the cart, you will probably bump into other people with carts. The rule is the same. Look ahead where you want to go.

Do not turn the wheel constantly

There are some inexperienced drivers and some misinformed ones who think that while driving, the wheel must always be moving. Consequently they are constantly turning the wheel back and forth. Some people get this mistaken notion from watching an actor drive on a movie screen. Actually, the actor is not driving. The movie screen is set up behind him showing scenery of a road. He moves the wheel to convey the illusion of driving.

If you are driving fast on a fairly straight road, the wheel is held almost motionless. If an adjustment is made, it should be hardly noticeable. When driving slower, the corrections would be more noticeable. The best drivers steer with a minimum of turning. By constantly over-steering, the inexperienced driver must turn more frequently to follow the road. If you are one of those who is always turning the wheel, hold it steadier and try to reduce your movements of the wheel. On a fairly straight road, do not turn the wheel too much. Usually a correction should be one sixteenth to one eighth of an inch. Turning more would cause oversteering.

<u>Holding the wheel in one position</u>

I have encountered this situation many times. I am teaching an older woman how to drive who has had no previous experience. She is starting out in a quiet area with no traffic. As she drives, I notice that she does not move the wheel at all. Eventually the car starts to drift to the side. When I tell her that she is not following the road, she is completely confused. She tells me that she can not understand why this is happening since she is not moving the wheel.

You must understand that the vehicle will not stay in your lane unless you guide your body towards the center of the lane. Most streets are not perfectly straight. Therefore, you must move the wheel slightly to follow the angle of the street.

Anyone who does not realize this could have a problem learning how to drive. This is a symptom of poor "motor skills".

Some neophyte drivers turn the wheel too much and others do not turn the wheel at all. If you have these problems after eight hours of driving, go through the test with the arrows on the ground. This is explained further in this chapter.

<u>People can give wrong advice</u>

This is a common scenario. A beginner goes out for a ride with a friend or relative. She is having a problem steering the car. The friend does not know how to help the learner. Accordingly, he tells her to do something he never does. He could tell her to watch the hood of the car or watch the right fender or watch the left front side of the car. The friend never drives using these ridiculous concepts, but in his eagerness to help, he is advising the learner incorrectly. I have heard these stories many times from people. As soon as they use their vision correctly, their steering problems disappear.

YOUNG PEOPLE LOSE FEAR QUICKLY

Some young people are almost as fearful about learning to drive as older people. However, they adapt themselves much quicker and after a few hours of driving their fears diminish. Older people must practice much longer and in most instances never completely lose their fear of driving.

DRIVING NEXT TO A CURB

Only an exceptional beginner can drive next to a curb or an island and stay precisely in the lane. When driving in the extreme, right lane, the beginners have a fear of going on the curb. They invariably will drive too far to the right or too far to the left either scraping the curb or interfering with vehicles on the left. The same problem exists when driving in the extreme left lane next to an island. New drivers could bear to the right and drive out of the lane. In these situations you must look in the center of the lane about forty or fifty yards away. Staring at the curb or island is a no-no.

Many times you will notice a dark streak about two feet wide in the center of the lane. This streak came from drops of oil from the cars. Looking at this streak will help especially on curves. Guide your body over the streaks and your vehicle will stay in the lane.

FIG. 3 - CAR IN MIDDLE OF LANE

If the street is straight and you are driving more than twenty-five miles per hour, you should look ahead at least one half block. Your eyes should be scanning near and far constantly. As long as your body is moving in the center of the lane, your vehicle will stay there. Do not stare at the island on your left. If a line of arrows were placed in the center of the lane, you would have no problem. Guiding your body over the arrows would keep your car exactly in the lane. Since there are no arrows, you must discipline yourself to look in the center of your lane. The same rule applies when driving in the extreme right lane. Do not stare at the curb. Alternate your vision by looking about twelve inches to the right of the line on your left (about forty yards away), and looking towards the center of the lane. Of course, when driving at a greater speed you will look further away.

Driving on curves

The sharper the curve, the closer you should look. When entering a curve, look in the center of the lane where the curve begins. Do not look beyond the curve. If you are coming to a curve to the left followed by a curve to the right you must look into the curve to the left first. Otherwise you will go to the right and miss the curve on the left.

FIG. 4 - DRIVING ON CURVES

Approach a curve slowly. You will have better traction in a curve if you do not brake while in the curve. If necessary use the brake before entering the curve and press the gas pedal slightly while in the curve. Do not look in the mirror just before entering the curve and while in the curve. Only an expert driver could do this and stay in the lane. When you enter a curve, you should have control of the car. Going too fast would make the car go out of the lane. You can not beat the laws of nature. Do not turn the wheel hand over hand on slight curves.

DRIVING ON ROADS WITH HIGH CROWNS

Many country roads are not flat. Some of them are high in the center and slope down at the sides. When driving on this type of road, you must grip the steering wheel tighter than usual. The force of gravity will pull the car to the right. By holding the wheel firmly, you can prevent the car from pulling to the right.

DRIVING ON NARROW ROADS

Two-lane narrow country roads with a solid yellow line in the center seems to be a common problem for young and old student drivers. They tend to gravitate too far to the right. On these rural roads the immediate space just inches to the right of the edge line may have jagged broken crevices and deep holes. Telegraph poles, just a foot off the road also present a possible hazard.

The new drivers will invariably steer too far to the right because they are afraid of the oncoming vehicles. The best way is to keep your left shoulder near the yellow line. Do not look down at the line too close to your vehicle. Doing this gives you the illusion that you are over the line when actually you might be inside your lane by at least two feet. When you mistakenly think you are over the line, you will usually turn too much to the right.

Look ahead about thirty yards to a point about one foot to the right of the yellow line. Try to keep your left shoulder moving towards this spot. Alternate your vision by also looking at the center of your lane about thirty or forty yards away. When a vehicle comes towards you, do not change your position. Do not move over to the right.

Do not stare at any vehicle coming towards you. Continue looking in the middle of your lane with your shoulder about one foot to the right of the yellow line. At a greater speed, you would have to look further away. I am assuming that an older driver would not be speeding on these rural roads, but would be moving about twenty to twenty -five miles per hour.

If you live in a rural area, you must be able to drive on these roads. Following the above instructions will help you drive safely.

STARING AT STOP SIGNS

The importance of looking ahead into your driving track can not be stressed enough. Neophyte drivers have a tendency to inadvertently allow their vision to stray. Some of them have a habit of staring at stop signs. As a result, the car will veer to the right even though the street could be angling to the left. Staring at stop signs can also cause your car to scrape parked cars on the right. Once you know the stop sign is there, do not stare at it. Look straight ahead while stopping at the intersection and you will stay in your lane.

Before looking left and right, look straight ahead and be sure you are staying in your lane. When you look left and right for an instant, do not move the wheel.

When crossing an intersection, you may find the street ahead of you curving to the left or right. If you are in the right lane, you must stay in the same lane when you cross over. Other vehicles may be on your left. If the street has marked lanes, you have to stay near the line on your left. If there are no marked lanes, look just past the intersection at the vehicle in front of you or approximately six feet from the curb. Guide your body towards that spot.

If you are on the left side or near the middle try to stay in the same lane. As you cross over try to keep your left shoulder near the center of the street. Do not look too far as you cross the intersection.

Many experienced drivers think that learning how to drive is easy. Most of them learned when they were young. Their "motor skills" were excellent so they had no problems learning how to steer. Ask anyone who tried to drive and failed. Some of them may say they were too nervous, but the truth is the majority of them could not learn to steer the car.

TESTS FOR STEERING

Practice going around circle
Find a small circular island in a quiet area. Try to go around the circle by always watching the center of the lane as the circle turns. If you are constantly veering towards the island, you are probably looking too long at the island.

FIG. 5-GOING AROUND CIRCLE

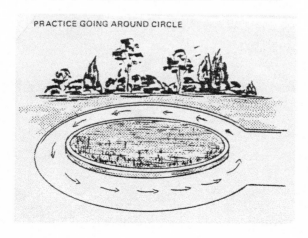

PRACTICE GOING AROUND CIRCLE

Take a piece of chalk and draw arrows on the ground as pictured in the illustration. Look at the arrows. Now you should have no difficulty going around the circle. It is amazing how much easier steering becomes when the beginner knows where to look.

Practice weaving in and out

Find an isolated area. Place six or seven objects on the ground about thirty-five feet apart. Use small cones or blocks of wood. They should be lined up straight. Now try to weave in and out between the objects at a speed of eight to ten miles per hour. Do not swing out too far. Look about three or four feet to the side of each object. Be sure to turn the wheel hand over hand. Do not look at the objects. If you do, you will drive over them.

If you are having difficulty with this steering exercise, there is one more thing you can do. Draw arrows on the ground about three feet to the side of each object. Place the first arrow at the left side of the next object. Place another arrow on the right side of the next object. Place arrows at the side of all the objects in this manner.

Now try it again. Look at the arrows and drive so your body goes over the arrows. If you can perform this exercise satisfactorily, you should be able to become a driver. However, if after practicing this procedure for eight hours and you still can not stay on the arrows, you may be one of the few who can not learn. Perhaps your motor skill is too subnormal for you to learn.

If you cannot steer a car precisely and cannot stay in a lane without drifting, you probably will never be able to drive. However, most people up to the age of seventy-two can become drivers, although many will be limited to residential areas. *If an aspiring slow learner shows a gradual improvement (no matter how slight) over a reasonable period of time, that learner will eventually learn to drive.* Expressways and turnpikes should be avoided. Of course, there are always exceptions.

<u>Doing multiple operations at the same time</u>

When competent drivers go on a busy highway or in the city on crowded streets, they can perform three or more operations simultaneously, and drive safely. They can look in the mirror, touch the brake, look for street signs and turn the wheel at the same time. While doing all of these things, they have no problem staying in the lane.

They do not have to look exclusively in the lane while driving the vehicle. Their experience allows them to glance quickly at all distractions and at the same time stay in the lane.

However, in the beginning most older people would probably have difficulty trying to perform too many operations at the same time. It is suggested that senior citizens stay out of heavy traffic or busy highways for at least one year. As you gain confidence, try to drive in heavier traffic, but do not force yourself if you do not feel comfortable.

<u>GUIDING YOUR BODY WITH YOUR EYES</u>

Some of my senior students did not readily understand the concept of guiding your body when driving a vehicle. When you are behind the steering wheel, you become part of the moving vehicle. Where your body goes the car will go. Therefore you must look ahead into the center of your driving path. When you look straight ahead and steer your body towards the center of your lane, you are guiding your car whether or not you are aware of it.

A woman once told me that her husband had been trying to teach her how to drive without success. She had driven with him for twenty hours. According to her, she had no trouble driving except she could not keep her vehicle from drifting. She knew how to go back and she could execute right turns and left turns.

I took her out in my driver training car. She got behind the wheel and immediately exclaimed, "I can not drive this car. It does not have a center piece on the front of the hood."

As soon as she said this, I knew why she could not stay in her lane. Her husband had told her to watch the center piece on the hood and line it up with the curb as she drove. As soon as I told her to look straight ahead, she kept the car in her lane. End of story.

CHAPTER 5
HOW TO GET STARTED

There are probably hundreds of thousands of people (mostly women) in the United States who have a valid driver's license but do not drive. In some instances, their husbands never encouraged them, others did not have automobiles and many were too scared. Of course, there are countless numbers of people who never tried.

Whether you have a friend teach you or if you go to a driving school, this book will serve as a valuable guide.

If you can afford it, go to a driving school. Stay away from any school which promises to teach you in one week or a school which promises to teach you in a few lessons.

Do not choose the largest school with the highest fees or a school with the lowest fees. Be sure the school you choose gives you private lessons. Some schools take two or three students out at one time.

Talk to people about driving schools. If you go to a beauty parlor, mention the subject to the beautician or other women. The chances are that someone there will recommend a driving school to you. A man can ask people at work, or he can ask his barber. Try to find someone who knows of a reliable school or a good instructor. If possible choose a smaller school which has been in the business for at least five years. Ask for an instructor who is patient and who has been teaching for at least five years.

The driving school you select is only as good as your instructor. There are excellent instructors and poor ones. An inexperienced instructor cannot cope with a slow learning older person who is nervous and timid. He does not have the experience and expertise to realize that the slow beginner will eventually blossom into a capable driver. Many women do not drive today because they were discouraged early by an impatient husband or an inexperienced driving instructor.

Patience, patience and more patience is the key, not only for the teacher, but also for the slow, timid learner. The teacher must not discourage the student and the student must not quit.

Some rural areas may not have driving schools. However, learning to drive in a rural area should be easier than learning in city traffic. If you do not have a driver's license, apply for a "learner's permit". Using this book as a guide, practice with a friend or relative. If possible do most of your driver training during daylight hours. One lesson should be at night.

STARTING THE ENGINE

Many new drivers are never taught how to start an automobile properly. If your vehicle has "fuel injection", you do not have to press the gas pedal before turning the ignition key. In a car with automatic transmission, the engine can only be started when the selector level is in "Park" or "Neutral". If the engine stalls when the lever is in "Drive" or "Reverse", you must place the lever back in "P" or "N" to restart the engine. "P" is preferable since the vehicle will not roll. Contrary to what many learners think, the car can roll when the lever is on "N" and the parking brake is not in effect.

It is important not to turn the key once the engine has started. Almost every learner at some time turns the key twice after the engine is already running. When I ask the beginners why they turned the key twice, the answer is always the same. They wanted to make sure the motor was on. Turning the key when the engine is already on can damage the "starter". Sometimes new drivers will say that they turned the key twice because they could not hear the engine. At times, there may be noise on the street so it would be difficult to hear the sound of the motor. To determine whether the engine is running, you must use your eyes as well as your ears. As you turn the key, red lights flash on the dash board (oil, charge, etc.). When the engine starts, the red lights go off. As soon as you turn the key look at the dash board. If the red lights go away, you know that the engine is running. Do not turn the key again.

Instead of turning the key while the indicator lever is in "Park", some learners move the lever to "Drive" and then turn the key. When nothing happens they are bewildered. The learner must remember that to start the engine, the key must be turned while the indicator lever is on "Park" or "Neutral".

Assume your vehicle does not have fuel injection and you are starting it on a cold day. Follow this procedure:

1.   Insert the key in the ignition. Do not force the key in the slot.

2.   Press the accelerator to the floor once or twice.

3.   Turn the key to the right as far as it goes. If the ignition slot is on the steering wheel, turn the key towards the front of the car.

4.   Do not press the accelerator while turning the key. Do not hold the key down for more than four or five seconds.

5.   If the engine does not start, press the accelerator again and turn the key once more.

On very cold days, let the engine idle for a few minutes before starting out. This will allow the oil to flow freely and the engine will operate more efficiently. If you are out shopping for an hour or so, it is not necessary to pump the accelerator to start the engine. If the engine is still warm, it should start by just turning the key. On warm summer days, most late model cars will start by turning the key without pressing the accelerator. Others may just need a slight pressure on the accelerator. The manual that comes with the car describes the best method for starting your car.

When you are taking lessons from a driving school, the engine is warm when you get behind the wheel. Therefore, you will not have to press the accelerator to start the engine. Some instructors tell you to start out with the engine already on. Tell him you want to start out with the ignition turned off so you can start the engine.

After you start the engine, it is imperative that you hold your right foot firmly on the brake when you are moving the indicator lever to "D" or "R". The vehicle will jump even if your foot is not on the accelerator, especially if your vehicle is idling fast.

Almost every new driver I have taught has at some time neglected to press the brake while changing gears. This is one of the most common mistakes made by beginners. Another common mistake made by beginners is forgetting to change the lever to "D" after going back in "R". Of course, when you are changing gears your foot must be held firmly on the brake pedal.

STARTING AN OLDER CAR

Not every automobile will start in the same manner as previously described. An older vehicle may not start readily, especially in cold weather. You may have to press the accelerator three or four times before turning the key. Turn the key all the way. Do not hold the key for more than three or four seconds. Holding the key down too long will injure the "starter". If the engine does not start, turn the key once more, perhaps pressing the accelerator once or twice will help.

After the engine starts, pat the accelerator gently for a few minutes. Never race the engine, especially when it is cold.

It is not uncommon for new drivers to turn the key the wrong way when turning off the ignition. Do not turn the key in the same direction when you turn it off as you did when you turned it on. If you do, you will hear an unnatural metallic sound which can damage the "starter".

If the ignition slot is on the steering column, turn the ignition off by turning the key towards the back of the vehicle. When the ignition slot is on the instrument panel, the key must always be turned back to the left in order to turn off the engine.

Do not try to force the key out of the ignition slot when you are finished. If the key does not come out easily, it is not in the proper groove. Either you turned the key back too far to the "Accessory" position or you did not turn it back far enough. The key should be turned back to "Lock" position for it to come out. When the ignition key is on the "Accessory" position, the motor is not running, but the electrical system is in effect. You can turn on the radio while the key is on the "ACC" position. Of course, you should not overdo this as it may drain the battery.

In many vehicles, the "Accessory" position may be located one notch below the "on" position. Some "Accessory" positions are situated below the "Lock" position.

HOW TO USE TURN SIGNALS

The small lever on the left side of the steering column operates the turn signals in the front and rear of the car. When you use the turn signals do not close your hand on the lever. To execute a right turn signal, put your fingers under the signal lever and push it up gently. If you grasp the lever in your fist and push too hard, you may break it.

For the left turn, put your fingers on top of the lever and push it down gently. On some cars, this same lever controls the headlights and high beam. On others, the lights and windshield wipers are located on the instrument panel. On many cars, (especially foreign) the windshield wipers are located on the right side of the steering column.

Nervousness sometimes causes the new driver to turn on the wrong turn signal. When executing a right turn, think of the word "upright". This will help you to remember to push the lever up for a right turn. The people I have taught have found this word association most helpful.

When a driver puts on a turn signal, a light flashes on the instrument panel. Most autos show arrows pointing right or left or a light flashes on the left or right side depending on which turn you are executing. At the same time, a signal light flashes in the front and rear of the vehicle, depending on which turn signal you are using. With a right signal, the signal flashes on the right side front and rear. With a left turn signal, the signal light flashes on the left side front and rear.

Turn signals should be put on well in advance. They are used so other drivers know beforehand what you are going to do. Turn signals are a method of communication between drivers.

In city traffic, execute the turn signals as soon as you pass the street before the one you are entering. Your signal should be on at least half a block before the intersection.

However, if there is a driver waiting in the driveway exit of a shopping market, do not put on the turn signal until you pass the driveway. The driver in the driveway may think you are entering the shopping section and may decide to move out into the street

When you are driving on a highway at a speed more than thirty-five miles per hour, you must use the turn signal much sooner. At a speed of fifty or fifty-five miles per hour, the signal should be put on about one thousand feet before the intersection or the equivalent of two city blocks.

Try to put on the turn signal at a red light or stop sign before you come to a stop. Putting on a turn signal after you stop can be very annoying to the drivers behind you.

HAND SIGNALS

Every driver should know how to use hand signals especially if the turn signals become defective. To signal for a left turn, point your left hand straight out so you are actually pointing to the left. Do not drop your hand until you start the turn. To signal for a right turn, point your left hand up over the top of the vehicle. Curve your hand towards the right and hold it there until you actually start executing the turn.

To signal that you are stopping, put your left hand out the window with your palm facing the vehicles behind you. Hold your hand lower than the window so that it will not be mistaken for a left turn signal.

Another hand signal that is important is motioning the drivers behind you to pass you if you intend to park your auto. Before you stop to park, wave to the drivers behind you to pass. Put your left hand out the window and rotate your hand in a circular clockwise forward motion. You should put on the hazard lights until you park your vehicle.

FIG. 6 - HAND SIGNALS

Left Turn　　　　Right Turn　　　　Stop

HOW TO USE THE BRAKE PEDAL

Before you drive in traffic, it is important to know how to use the brake pedal. Choose an empty parking lot or a quiet area to practice.

In a car with automatic transmission, the right foot is used for the brake pedal and the accelerator (gas pedal).

Every motor vehicle must have an emergency brake—sometimes called a parking brake. There are two types of parking brakes. Usually larger cars have the emergency brake on the extreme left side of the car. It resembles a small brake pedal which rests near your left foot about six inches from the floor. When you are parking the car, you press this pedal with your left foot. To start driving, you pull out a small lever which usually rests just below the dash board above the emergency brake. A red warning light appears on the instrument panel if you forget to release the emergency brake when the car is moving. Failure to release the parking brake will eventually cause the brake lining to melt down and you will notice a burning odor. The car will also appear sluggish.

The other type of parking brake is a rod which rests on the floor between the two front seats of the vehicle. Small cars and sports cars usually have this type of parking brake. When parking the car, you pull the rod up. When beginning to drive, you press a small knob at the top of the rod. You do not have to push the knob when you are pulling the rod up to park. You only push the knob to release it.

When parking the car use the parking brake and put the indicator lever in "P" so the transmission will be locked. A car with automatic transmission will not roll if you put the lever on Park. If you only put on the emergency brake, the car could possibly roll if it was not set tight enough. Therefore, it is important to use both when parking the vehicle. The emergency brake should also be used if the regular brake malfunctions.

Every time you step on the regular brake pedal, the brake lights in the rear of the car light up. The motor does not have to be running for the brake lights to go on.

When your right foot is using the accelerator, your heel must rest on the floor. To switch to the brake pedal, lift your foot from the accelerator and place the ball of your foot on the brake pedal. Do not keep your heel on the floor while using the brake pedal. Do not keep your heel on the floor when switching from the brake pedal to the gas pedal. Lift your foot every time.

Start the engine. Hold your right foot firmly on the brake pedal while moving the indicator lever from "P" to "D". Release the emergency brake. Before beginning, be sure the mirrors are adjusted for you.

If you never drove before, you probably will have a tendency to step on the brake pedal too hard. Looking straight ahead, touch the gas pedal softly so the vehicle is moving about ten miles an hour. Now test the brake pedal. Place your right foot on the brake pedal with a firm, gentle pressure. As the car is stopping, release most of the pressure from the brake pedal. When you feel that the car is stopping, do not press down on the brake. If the car jerks when it stops, you pressed too hard. The car will send you a message every time you press too hard on the brake pedal.

You will observe that when you are moving slowly, the brake pedal does not need much pressure to stop the car. If you are not stopping smoothly, continue practicing until the car stops without jerking. Do not be discouraged if you are not successful in the beginning. When you start to relax, you will improve.

The faster the car is moving, the sooner you use the brake pedal. Many inexperienced drivers wait to long to use the brake. Therefore, when they reach the red light, they have to press hard to stop the car and the car stops with a sudden jerk. The best way to stop smoothly at a speed of thirty miles per hour is to start pressing the brake in the middle of the block. Squeeze the brake firmly and hold it down until you are moving about ten or fifteen miles an hour. Do not jab the brake quickly. As you are stopping, pretend you are stepping on a soft boiled egg and you do not want to crack the shell. Remember that as the car stops the pressure of your foot must be restrained.

IMPORTANT FACTS ABOUT USING THE BRAKE

1.   The faster you are going, the sooner you use the brake.

2.   Do not use the brake suddenly.

3.   Do not hesitate to use the brake hard to prevent an accident.

4.   Do not jab at the brake. Squeeze it firmly.

5.   Use the brake sooner when going down a slope even if the traffic signal is green.

6.   Do not use the brake excessively. Remember when you press the brake pedal the brake lights go on in the rear.

CHAPTER 6
PREPARATION FOR DRIVING

If you wanted to become a good golfer, you would first have to learn how to hold the golf club; how to swing the club; where to look, etc. This is also true of tennis, baseball, bowling and almost every other physical activity. In most activities, eye concentration is extremely important. When driving an automobile, total eye concentration is more important because people's lives are at stake.

Before you begin to drive alone in traffic, you should be proficient in the following:

1. Correct use of your vision
2. Right turns and left turns
3. Reverse
4. Braking
5. Steering
6. Road signs and traffic rules

The above six categories are basic requisites for all drivers.

DRIVING POSTURE

When you sit behind the wheel, you should feel comfortable. Your right knee should be slightly bent as you touch the accelerator. When you use the brake pedal, your right knee will be bent more since the brake is higher than the accelerator.

If you are shorter than five feet three inches, you will probably need cushions to sit closer and higher. Your line of vision should be at least two inches above the top of the steering wheel. Never look under the top of the wheel when driving a car. There are some short people who actually do this. This seriously impairs your vision. Your elbows should be down and slightly bent, not too close to the body and not too close to the steering wheel. The following procedures should be applied every time you are about to drive:

1.   Fasten your seat belt. Keep the lap belt below your abdomen and not above your hips.

2.   Adjust your seat.

3.   Adjust the rear mirror and the left side mirror.

4.   After you start the motor release the parking brake.

5.   Always check traffic behind you before moving.

Sit as straight as you can. Do not slouch and do not lean back. Unless you are shorter than five feet two inches, your body should not be too close to the steering wheel.

You must look straight ahead directly over the center of the steering wheel. Do not look at the center of the car. Look eye level straight ahead into the center of your driving path.

The rear view mirror should be adjusted so you can see about five hundred feet behind you. The left side mirror should be adjusted so you can see as far as possible on your left side or at least a city block. You should be able to see any car alongside of you on your left.

HAND OVER HAND TURNING

Turning the wheel hand over hand is the most efficient method for turning around corners or anytime when a lot of turning is necessary. Many people driving today do not use this method. They turn the wheel with short, awkward movements and have to turn the wheel many more times.

These people either are self taught or were taught incorrectly. They drifted into the wrong method without realizing the importance of hand over hand turning. It is impossible to turn the wheel quickly any other way. It could also be dangerous. Turning the wheel hand over hand enables the driver to have complete control when executing right and left turns.

However, some nervous new drivers do not turn hand over hand because they are afraid to let go of the wheel. Using hand over hand, one hand releases the wheel while the other hand turns. You should never turn the wheel at the same time with two hands.

Climbing up a rope is not exactly the same as turning a steering wheel, but using two hands while rope climbing is almost impossible. Trying to turn a wheel with two hands at the same time is extremely awkward and inefficient. The only time hand over hand is not necessary is when you have to turn the wheel once in order to go around a curve or turn into a street that is slightly curved so only one turn is required.

Some people adapt to hand over hand turning easily while others have difficulty mastering it. By persevering everyone should be able to learn hand over hand turning.

Imagine the steering wheel is a clock.

FIG. 7 - HAND POSITIONS ON WHEEL

Normal hand position for driving.

Hand positions on wheel

Your left hand should hold the wheel at nine or ten o'clock. Your right hand should hold the wheel at two or three o'clock. Hold the wheel firmly as you would hold a baby. You should feel comfortable.

Some people have a tendency to keep their hands down at the bottom of the wheel. In this position, hand over hand turning would be difficult. Try to remember to keep your hands up above the center of the wheel. Hand over hand turning will come more easily if your hands are in the correct position.

FIG. 8 - HAND-OVER-HAND TURNING

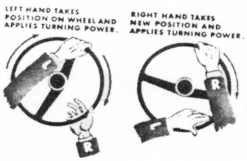

Practice "U" Turns

A good exercise to master hand over hand turning is to begin by making "U" turns to the right and to the left. Find an empty space that is seldom used.

Let's assume you are going to practice "U" turns going to the left. When turning to the left for a "U" turn or a left turn, start the turn with your right hand.

Hand Over Hand Technique

1.   When you begin, your right hand should be at two o'clock and your left hand should be placed at ten

o'clock. Turn the wheel to the left with your right hand until your right hand reaches eleven o'clock.

2.	As your right hand begins to turn, you must release the wheel with your left hand.

3.	When your right hand turns the wheel to eleven o'clock, put your left hand on the wheel at one o'clock.

4.	Release your right hand and turn the wheel to the left with your left hand to 10 o'clock. At the same time, place your right hand on the right side of the wheel without gripping it so it is ready to turn. Continue turning in this hand over hand manner until you cannot turn the wheel anymore. While you are waiting for the vehicle to face in the opposite direction in which you started from, be sure to look straight ahead. At this point do not keep your hands on the same side of the wheel. Hold your left hand on the left side of the wheel and the right hand on the right side of the wheel.

5.	When you are ready to straighten out, turn the wheel back hand over hand two times or whatever is necessary. Steering wheels on some vehicles snap back faster than you can turn. If the wheel on your vehicle snaps back very quickly, release your grip on the wheel when you are facing straight ahead and let the wheel snap back. Do not watch the front of the vehicle. As always you must

LEFT HAND TAKES
POSITION ON WHEEL AND
APPLIES TURNING POWER.

RIGHT HAND TAKES
NEW POSITION AND
APPLIES TURNING POWER.

look straight ahead. Grip the wheel again when you are facing straight. Only straighten out in this manner if you can handle it safely. Otherwise turn the wheel back in the hand over hand method.

It is very important not to push the gas pedal while you are practicing this exercise. Most of the time your car will roll slowly when in "D" or "R" position. If somehow the car does not move slowly without touching the gas pedal, be sure to touch the pedal very lightly as you practice the "U" turns. Inexperienced drivers should never push the gas pedal too much when turning corners or making "U" turns. The faster the turn is made, the more skill is needed to straighten out the car. After you have been driving approximately six months, you may be able to let the wheel spin back safely and keep the car in its proper place. A driver must accelerate in order to let the wheel spin back. New middle-aged drivers are usually not ready for this. Stepping on the gas pedal too much while turning corners has caused many accidents for new drivers. New drivers should execute all turns slowly, never more than five miles per hour.

When you make the "U" turn to the right, you turn the wheel in the same manner as you do when going to the left, except you start turning the wheel with your left hand.

You begin with your left hand at ten o'clock and your right hand at two o'clock. Turn the wheel to the right with your left hand until your left hand reaches one or two o'clock. As your left hand turns the wheel, you release your grip on the wheel with your right hand. Place your right hand on the wheel at eleven o'clock and turn the wheel to two o'clock. At the same time you release the wheel with your left hand. Continue turning in this manner until you cannot turn the wheel anymore. As explained before, wait until you are facing in the opposite direction. At this point look straight ahead and turn the wheel back two or three times. This should be enough to straighten out. By looking straight ahead, you should know how much to turn the wheel back in order to go straight. Try to do this without touching the gas pedal. The car should roll unless you are on an upgrade. Do not go into city traffic until you have mastered hand over hand turning together with right and left turns.

CHAPTER 7
REGULATORY SIGNS - COMMON SENSE RULES

Regulatory signs tell you what to do or what not to do. These signs have black or red markings on a white background. Signs with black markings tell you what you must do. For example, signs giving speed limits and lane use instructions have black markings on a white background.

Some signs have a black symbol in a red circle, crossed by a red bar. The red bar and circle show what you cannot do.

Some regulatory signs have a special shape and color. For example, there is the "STOP SIGN", "YIELD", "DO NOT ENTER", "WRONG WAY", "ONE WAY" and "RAILROAD CROSSBUCK SIGNS".

The "STOP" sign is red octagon, or eight- sided figure with white markings. This sign means you have to stop at the stop line, or before the crosswalk if there is no stop line. Before proceeding, yield to all traffic that does not have to stop.

The "YIELD" sign is a red and white triangle pointing down. This sign warns you that you should slow down, but need not stop unless other vehicles are crossing in front of you. Do not interfere with the progress of other drivers. If other drivers are approaching, you must stop.

The "WRONG WAY" sign is a red horizontal rectangle. When you see this sign do not enter the road. If you make a mistake and have entered the road, go off the road quickly and change direction as soon as the way is clear.

The "DO NOT ENTER" sign is a white square with a red circle. Inside the red circle is a white bar with the words, DO NOT ENTER. You must not enter any road where this sign appears.

A "ONE WAY" sign is a black rectangle with a white arrow that shows the direction you can drive on the roadway.

The "RAILROAD CROSSBUCK" is a white X-shaped sign with black lettering. It warns you that a railroad crossing is ahead. Slow down and prepare to stop for a train when you see this sign.

WARNING SIGNS

Warning signs tell you about possible dangers ahead. Whenever you see one, be prepared to slow down or stop. Most warning signs are yellow diamonds with black legends. They contain symbols or words.

A few warning signs have different shapes or colors. SCHOOL CROSSING and SCHOOL ZONE signs are yellow pentagons (five sided figures) with black legends. Slow down and be prepared to stop when you see these signs.

The RAILROAD CROSSING ahead sign is round and has a yellow background with a black legend. Be prepared to stop for trains when you see this sign. This sign may be accompanied with a flashing red light when a train is approaching. Do not go when the red light is flashing.

Road construction, repair and detour signs are always orange with black legends. They may be diamond shaped or rectangular. These signs are often found on expressway ramps, before curves and in other areas requiring a change in speed.

GUIDE SIGNS

Information about location, direction, types of services available, or points of interest is given on GUIDE SIGNS.

These signs are usually square or rectangular and have color-coded messages.

Destination and distance signs are green with white legends. They provide you with information about route directions and the distance from one place to another.

Milepost signs are also green with white numerals. These signs are placed along the roadway at one-mile intervals.

Rest, scenic and service area signs are blue with white legends. These tell you where to find such services as service stations, hospitals, restaurants and telephones. Recreation area signs are brown with white legends.

A <u>ROUTE MARKER</u> always tells the number of the highway. The shape and color of the marker depend on the kind of highway. An interstate highway is marked by a red and blue shield. A green shield shows an interstate business route.

PAVEMENT MARKINGS

Pavement markings are the yellow or white markings painted directly onto the road surface. They help to regulate traffic, define lanes and warn drivers of possible dangers.

EDGE LINES

Edge lines are solid white lines along the side of the road that mark the outside edge of the road. Edge lines do not continue through intersections, so their absence helps you to identify intersections.

BROKEN LINE

You may cross a broken line if ample passing distance exists.

SOLID AND BROKEN LINE

Permits crossing from one side only if enough passing distance exists. Pass only if broken line is on your side of the highway. Solid lines indicate that you may not cross into the other lane.

SOLID YELLOW LINES

Solid yellow lines separate traffic moving in opposite directions. It is illegal to cross a solid yellow line except when you are entering or leaving a roadway or making a legal turn. The solid line prohibits vehicles to the right of it from crossing the line to pass. A double solid yellow line indicates that passing is illegal for vehicles on either side of the highway.

FIVE-LANE ROADS

Some two-way roads have five lanes. The middle lane has solid yellow lines on both sides. Usually broken yellow lines are inside the solid lines. The center lane is used for left turns for vehicles going in both directions. If you want to execute a left turn, enter the middle lane when you are near the intersection or near the point where you wish to turn left. Do not enter the middle lane prematurely since a vehicle coming towards you may enter the same lane. The middle lane should only be used for left turns.

DIAGONAL LINES

Diagonal lines could be on your right or left. Do not drive or park your vehicle on diagonal lines.

If you ever are confused about signs, pavement markings or traffic signals that you may encounter, ask an experienced driver for an explanation.

TRAFFIC SIGNALS

Traffic-control signals are used to help keep traffic moving in an orderly way. Red means stop; yellow, proceed with caution and prepare to stop; green, go if the way is clear.

Traffic lights may be located on a support at the side of the road or suspended above the middle of an intersection. They can be arranged horizontally or vertically. Red is on the top in a vertical arrangement and to the left in a horizontal one. Yellow is always in the middle, green is at the bottom of a vertical arrangement and at the right of a horizontal one.

COMMON SENSE RULES

Most rules of the road are the same all over the United States. For new drivers these are the important ones:

1.   On a two-way road, always drive right of the center. If you are on a one-way road, you may drive on either side, but do not straddle the lane;

2.   If you are a slow driver, always stay in the extreme right lane. Be sure to drive at least at the minimum speed that is posted;

3.   When two vehicles enter an intersection not controlled by a signal or sign, the driver on the left should yield to the one on the right;

4.   When you approach a four-way stop sign first, yield to any driver on your left or right if that driver is very aggressive;

5.   If you intend to turn left at an intersection, you must yield to oncoming traffic unless you have a left green arrow;

6.   If you are turning right and a vehicle coming towards you at the same time is turning left, you should go first. If the one turning left is aggressive, wait and go after the aggressive driver;

7.   Yield to pedestrians and other vehicles when coming out of a driveway;

8.   When stopping at an intersection for a red traffic signal, you do not have to pass the white line to see if the way is clear. The traffic signal is controlling traffic. When the traffic signal changes to green, be sure vehicles on your left and right are stopping before you proceed;

9.   A posted speed limit is the speed recommended under good conditions. When driving during inclement weather or in extremely dark areas, you should drive slower than usual. You must have control of the vehicle;

10.   If you are driving in a strange area, slow down at intersections so you will know where the stop signs are. Do not cross intersections unless you know who has the right to go first.

11.   If you are about to enter a traffic circle, you must yield to all vehicles already going around the circle.

CHAPTER 8
RIGHT TURNS AND TIGHT SPACES

It usually takes longer for nervous learners and older people to master right and left turns since good coordination is required. When turning, sometimes it is necessary to turn the wheel while touching the brake pedal. Other times the driver may have to touch the accelerator while turning the wheel. In the beginning it may be difficult for the older driver since she or he has to perform more than one operation when turning. Therefore, the most ideal situation would be when the learner can turn without touching the brake or the accelerator. Accordingly, this can only be done from a stopped position when the car rolls by itself.

STAY OUT OF TRAFFIC

Find a quiet area which has a stop sign on every corner. You are going to make right turns at every street, so after making four right turns you will be where you originally started. Now when you make each right turn, you can relax more since you will begin from a stopped position. As long as the ground is level, the vehicle will roll without touching the gas pedal.

START WITH LEFT HAND

You should always start the right turn with your left hand. Starting with your right hand would be awkward since your right hand would have to be taken off the wheel and placed at the top of the wheel in order to turn. This would take two movements. The smoother method is to begin by turning the wheel with your left hand. Do not lift your left hand away from the wheel before you turn.

Conversely, the same rules apply when making a left turn except you begin with your right hand.

TAKE TWO OR THREE TURNS

Most people under five feet three inches tall would usually need three hand movements for a right turn. Therefore, starting with the left hand, it would be LEFT, RIGHT, LEFT. However, the number of times you turn really depends on how far you turn the wheel. Taller people who take longer strokes can turn using two hand movements, which would be LEFT, RIGHT. A very tiny person who is also timid might have to turn four times. Slanting the vehicle to the right at the corner is especially important to the small learner as it will decrease the number of hand movements she or he will need.

HOW TO PRACTICE RIGHT TURNS

At the intersection, start out from the stop sign. Always look to your left before making a right turn. Yield to any vehicle on your left before making a right turn. Yield to any vehicle on your left if there is no stop sign for the driver on your left.

Your car should be on a slight angle about three feet from the curb, but do not stare at the curb. If you do not slant the car, you may go out too straight and the turn will be too wide.

Line up windshield

Take your foot away from the brake pedal and allow the car to roll until the windshield is lined up with the end of the curb. Before turning, your left hand should be at ten o'clock and your right hand at two o'clock.

FIG. 9- RIGHT TURNS

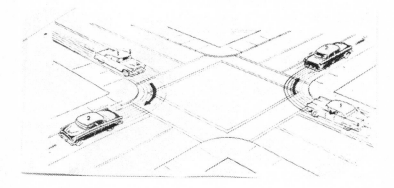

<u>Look where the arrows appear</u>

At this point, turn the wheel with your left hand to one o'clock, bring your right hand to eleven o'clock, and turn the wheel to two o'clock. If you slanted the car before the turn, you should not have to turn the wheel anymore. If you are taking smaller strokes when turning, you would need one more turn.

<u>When to turn back</u>

Many beginners do not know when to straighten out after turning around the corner. More often they turn the wheel back too soon especially if there are parked cars on the right. The accuracy of the turn depends mainly on where you are looking as you turn. First, you must look into the center of your turning path as shown by the arrows on the illustration. After turning the wheel two or three times, you must wait until you are facing straight ahead on the same angle as the street. <u>Do not press</u> the accelerator. This is very important. You must move slowly. When you are more experienced, you will be able to touch the gas pedal while turning. If you press the gas pedal at this time, you may lose control and possibly ride up on the curb.

Now turn the wheel back approximately two times. At this time, do not look far away. Look about twenty feet in front of you. Be sure you are looking in the center of your lane. As you turn, your eyes should be aiming low (at the arrows). As soon as you feel you are moving straight ahead, raise your vision so that you are looking ahead two hundred feet or half of a city block.

Never watch front of car

Under no circumstances are you to look at the front of your car while turning or when completing the turn. Always remember that when you drive, you guide your body not the car.

If some beginners are not told to turn a certain number of times they turn the wheel until it can not be turned anymore. If they step on the accelerator too much while oversteering, the results could be disastrous.

When you begin the right turn, it should take you about two to three seconds to complete the two or three turns. If you turn the wheel too slowly, the car will swing out too far to the left side of the street.

Some people turn the wheel too slowly because they think that if the car is moving slowly, the wheel should be turned slowly. This is not true. There are times when a driver is going faster, but moves the wheel slowly and there are times when the car is moving slowly while the wheel must be turned quickly.

Do not let wheel spin back

Almost every experienced driver lets the wheel spin back to straighten out after a turn. Many new drivers, especially senior citizens are not capable of letting the wheel spin back after a turn. The wheel will not spin back if the car is moving very slowly or if the driver's foot is pressing down on the brake pedal. The car should be moving freely or accelerated for the wheel to spin back. This procedure could be dangerous for the neophyte driver, yet some books on driving actually recommend this method. Not only must the driver accelerate, but she or he must know when to release the grip as well as when to hold the wheel again. This is too much to expect from an older person or a nervous learner.

I have no doubt that these books on driving have been written by eminent people well known in the driving field. However, I doubt whether they have actually taught older or frightened beginners how to drive. Most new drivers have to drive for a few months before they can let the wheel spin back correctly.

Could a first year violinist play a difficult concerto by Vivaldi or Bach? The new violinist would have to practice for three to five years before attempting this music. Therefore, a new or older driver should not be expected to perform as well as someone who has been driving for five or ten years.

<u>Older people have difficulty absorbing</u>

Years ago, I was teaching a sixty-eight year old woman how to make right turns. I told her many times where to look when making a right turn. I thought she understood me,. but for some reason, she made the turns poorly. Finally after a particularly bad turn, I asked her where she was looking. To my amazement, she pointed to a red car which was parked to our left in a driveway. This was after six hours of driving lessons in which I patiently told her where to look when making a right turn.

With a piece of chalk I drew three arrows at the corner showing her where to look. One arrow was curved in the center of the turning path and the other two were pointed straight ahead as shown in the illustration. When she made the turn looking at the arrows, it was almost magical how her turns improved.

This was not an isolated incident. There are many reasons some older people cannot follow instructions. No doubt nervousness and lack of confidence hampers them. There was one older woman in particular who had a mental block about going backwards. Her instincts would not allow her to turn the wheel in the proper direction when she used Reverse. She insisted on turning the wheel the way she wanted the front to go. When this happened, I would tell her which way to turn the wheel. I told her she was wrong and pointed in the direction I wanted her to turn. In spite of this she continued to turn the wheel the wrong way. When I questioned her she admitted that she had a mental block about reverse. When I told her to pretend the back of the car was the front, she mastered reverse.

Place arrows on ground

If you are not executing right or left turns properly after six hours of practice, place arrows on the ground as illustrated in this chapter. Practice going over the arrows. Fix your vision on the first arrow and drive so your body goes over the arrow. Straighten out so your body goes over the next arrow. Be sure to go slowly as you go over the arrows. People who have steering problems are usually so nervous that they cannot look straight ahead. They are too easily distracted by the motion of their car or side objects. Placing arrows on the ground helps them train their eyes to look in the center of the lane. After enough practice their nervousness should diminish.

Make turns slowly

Beginners should never make right turns more than five miles an hour. Driving at a speed of twenty miles an hour is not fast for straight driving. However, if you try to turn a corner at this speed, the vehicle would veer out of control, especially in the hands of a beginner. When you turn right or left you are fighting a law of nature. The vehicle is going straight and you are trying to change its direction. A young driver with excellent "motor skills" senses this and will instinctively squeeze the brake hard enough to slow the car's momentum sufficiently to make the turn safely. However, the middle-aged learner or anyone having difficulty learning may not know how to cope with this situation. They may not press the brake hard enough for fear of stopping suddenly or they may not realize that the car is going too fast to turn safely. Some may think that not touching the accelerator will slow down the car's momentum. In this situation the brake must be used. If the street is going downhill, the brake pedal must be pressed harder. The driver with good "motor skills" will press the brake enough, but the person with poor "motor skills" will not have a "feel" for the car and could lose control. It has been proven that "motor skills" can be improved. I have seen it happen with the people I have taught to drive.

When you are making a turn at a corner after you have stopped for a red light or a stop sign, do not keep your foot on the brake when executing the turn. Let the car glide or touch the accelerator softly if the car does not move. When approaching an intersection for a right turn and the light is green, slow down to less than ten miles an hour. If you are going faster, squeeze the brake enough so the car does not swing over into the left side of the street. However, if you misjudge your brake pressure and you feel the car is stopping, take your foot away from the brake pedal and the car will move. It is better not to push the accelerator at this time because the tendency will be to press too hard.

Turning back too soon

This is a problem almost all new drivers have. When making right and left turns, they tend to turn the wheel back too soon after the turn is made. If the wheel is turned back too soon on a right turn, the vehicle will veer to the left. If the wheel is turned back too soon on a left turn, the vehicle will veer to the right. In either instance, these errors could cause an accident with either a parked car, oncoming traffic or another vehicle on the side.

Straightening out too soon is a common mistake even with new young drivers. When practicing, look straight ahead after the turn and turn back the wheel when you are facing straight ahead. Do not look far when turning back the wheel.

<u>Tight spaces</u>

Most new drivers dread the thought of driving through narrow spaces. A good example of this is when a right turn has to be made on a small street with a car parked around the corner. The street has four lanes, but the extreme lane on the left and the extreme lane on the right is for parked cars. That means that you have to drive in the lane next to the cars on the right.

FIG. 10-RIGHT TURN IN TIGHT SPACES

On a slant, turn the wheel when windshield is parallel to the left rear end of parked car.

Assume that you are waiting at the intersection for the red signal to change to green. When the signal light changes to green, take your foot from the brake and let the car glide without touching the accelerator. Turn the wheel so the car slants slightly to the right. Do not touch the accelerator unless the car does not move. If this happens, touch the gas pedal very softly. Allow the car to go out on a slant until the windshield of your car is parallel to the outer left end of the parked car. Do not stare at the left rear end of the parked car once you have your windshield parallel to it. Since you have already slanted the car, you should only have to turn the wheel two times. As you turn aim low into the center of the lane next to the parked car. After you make the turn, look straight ahead about half a block into the center of your lane. Do not stare at any vehicles coming towards you. Do not stare at the parked cars.

Guide your body

Always remember the key to driving. When driving through a tight space, guide your body into the center of your lane. The car will automatically move into your lane. After you do this correctly, you will have more confidence with this kind of situation.

If you slant the car before executing a right turn, you should only need two or two and a half turns. Slanting the car enough is equivalent to one turn. Sometimes when you turn the wheel back you may not need two turns. Be sure you do not slant the car to the right too soon. The car should be slanted at the time the front of the car is parallel with the end of the curb. As you drive, you will get a "feel" for turning and you will make the proper adjustment. Practice, practice, practice.

Right turns on red lights

You are permitted to make a right turn on a red light under the following conditions:

1.   When there is no sign facing you which reads "No Turn on Red".

2.   There should be no traffic coming from your left side.

3.   You must pause at the intersection before turning.

4.   There should be no pedestrians crossing the street.   If all of these conditions are prevalent, you can make a right turn on red.   However, if you don't want to turn on red, you don't have to.   You can wait for the traffic signal to turn to green.   If a sign on your left or right side (not facing you) reads "No Turn on Red", you may turn on red as long as the sign does not face you.   The "No Turn on Red" must be facing you, otherwise it is not for you.

Repetition helps

I have gone into detail explaining how to make "U" turns and right turns.   In fact, the explanations appear redundant especially to anyone who knows how to drive. After many years of teaching many middle-aged people and younger fearful students, I have found it very helpful and necessary to give repetitive and methodical instructions. After fifty and sixty many people become hesitant about trying something new especially where coordination and an element of danger is involved.

Right green arrows

Some traffic signals may have a green arrow pointing to the right.   This means that you can turn right even though the traffic control signal is red.   If the green arrow is pointing to the left or straight ahead, you are not permitted to execute a right turn.

CHAPTER 9
LEFT TURNS AND CIRCLES

Left turns can be more hazardous than right turns because of oncoming traffic. However, by knowing the rules and driving defensively, left turns can be executed safely.

The following basic rules should be followed:

1. Do not move faster than five miles per hour.
2. Vehicle should be placed near center lane two blocks in advance.
3. Turn signal should be used three quarters of a block before intersection (city driving).
4. Never slant the vehicle while going to center of intersection for left turn. (City driving)
5. Proceed only if traffic is clear of oncoming traffic and intersecting traffic.
6. Do not hurry the turn. Turning the wheel quickly does not make the car go faster.
7. Do not turn the wheel more than two or three times.
8. As you start to turn look into the street you are entering to help you steer correctly and to see if it is free of pedestrians.
9. Check for traffic over your left shoulder when turning.
10. Do not turn left where it is illegal. This is a moving violation which will hurt your pocket book and your driving record. In some states, you may be required to take a driving examination if you have more than two moving violations in one year. Failure to pass the examination may result in the loss of your driver's license.
11. Be sure to wait for traffic to clear when only you have a stop sign.

12.   At four-way stop signs, do not turn left if the other driver approaches aggressively. It is safer to yield.

Start left turns with right hand

The mechanics of a left turn are similar to that of a right turn except you start with your right hand. Of course, you use the hand over hand method. Most left turns should only require two turns of the wheel, especially on a wide street.

You begin with your left hand at nine or ten o'clock and your right hand at two or three o'clock. When beginning to turn, it is important not to lift your right hand from the wheel. Do not move it to another spot on the wheel before turning. Older people seem to be more prone to do this. Begin to turn by moving the wheel with your right hand from two o'clock to eleven o'clock. As you release your right hand from the wheel, turn the wheel with your left hand from two o'clock to ten o'clock. The wheel should now be turned sufficiently for you to execute the left turn. All that remains is to turn back the wheel a few times to go straight

Left turns at stop sign

Assume you are approaching a stop sign and you want to make a left turn. You have already put on your left signal so all other drivers know what you want to do. Come to a complete stop at the stop sign. Now roll out slightly so you can see at least one block to your left and your right. There are no cars coming from either direction. However, there is a car coming towards you. This driver also has a stop sign. Because you are making a left turn, you should yield to the driver coming towards you. After this car passes, you can make the left turn provided the street you are turning into is still free of approaching vehicles.

Glance left and right again, and if the street is clear, go straight out to the middle of the street. Before you start turning, glance again in front of you to be sure no car is approaching. When your body starts to pass the middle of the street, turn your head towards the street you are entering. At this time, you look into the center of your turning path to your left. Turning your head at this time will prevent you from making the turn too wide. After the turn is completed, you should look ahead about two hundred feet. Do not accelerate until you have straightened out. Guide yourself into the lane just right of the center if you are practicing on a quiet street. When you are driving onto a busy street, you should steer over into the lane on the right. Be sure to put on your right signal and check traffic on your right before moving over.

When making a left turn into a wide street, you should find it necessary to only turn the wheel two times. Start the turn with your right hand and follow with your left hand. On narrow streets, you may have to turn three times which would be RIGHT, LEFT, RGHT.

Turning left into traffic

Turning left at busy intersections can be frightening for new drivers, especially senior citizens. However, once this is mastered, it will pose no problem.

Suppose you are waiting for the traffic signal to turn to green. Your left signal is flashing and your car is just right of the center. When the light turns to green, you roll out slowly to the middle of the street. You do not slant the car to the left. You stay STRAIGHT. If you slant your car, you will interfere with oncoming traffic. Drivers behind you will pass you on your right because they know you are trying to turn left. If cars are coming towards you, wait in the middle of the street. When no cars are coming towards you, you may complete the turn.

FIG. 11 TURNING LEFT INTO TRAFFIC.

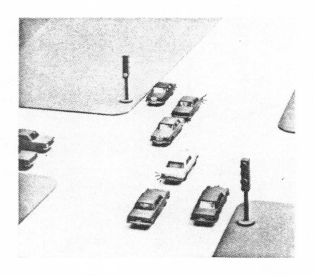

Look out for hidden cars coming towards you before turning left. If the oncoming traffic is extremely heavy, you will have to turn left when the traffic signal turns to red. At this position you cannot stay in the middle of the street because you will block the intersection. Do not proceed until the cars coming towards you have stopped. If you notice an oncoming car speeding, <u>do not turn</u>. It is not unusual for drivers to speed through red lights in this instance. Neophyte middle-aged drivers usually get very nervous when faced with this predicament. Remember that the drivers to your left and right at the intersection see you and they realize they have to wait for you. They may get annoyed because you are moving slowly, but your purpose is to drive safely. With more experience, this procedure will be a piece of cake. Every driver is faced with this situation and it is imperative for every new driver to know how to execute a left turn in heavy traffic.

Look to the left before turning

When you are waiting in the middle of an intersection to make a left turn, glance towards the street you are turning into. Observe if any pedestrians are crossing the street. Do not proceed if anyone is walking even though no vehicles are approaching. Remember that pedestrians have the right of way, especially in this instance.

Oversteering

The new driver usually gets flustered when making a left turn into heavy traffic. The immediate reaction is to turn the wheel too quickly and all the way. Turning the wheel quickly does not move the vehicle faster. Only pressing the accelerator moves the vehicle faster. Turning the wheel all the way will make the car move too far to the left, especially if the accelerator is pushed too hard. This could be hazardous.

The object is to move the car slowly (about five miles per hour). No matter how anxious you are, you must turn the wheel the usual two or three times. Turn the wheel back when you are facing straight ahead. If the vehicle is rolling, do not touch the accelerator. Do not touch the brake pedal as the car may stop or move too slowly. As you turn, look down into your turning path until you are facing straight ahead. Now you should look straight ahead eye level for one half to one block ahead. After you get more experience and confidence, you will be able to control left turns with a little more speed.

Have patience and try not to allow other drivers to rattle you. The streets are filled with impatient drivers. Do not let any of them force you to rush your turns. You cannot drive the way they want you to drive. You must drive with the car under your control. Think about it. If you are involved in an accident while turning, you will at the very least be partially responsible. In many accidents at intersections both drivers are responsible.

<u>Turning left on one way streets</u>

When turning left from a one-way street to a two-way street, stay on the extreme left lane, but go out half way into the two-way street before turning the wheel. Be sure when you turn that you guide yourself to the right half of the street you are entering.

If the street facing you has become a two-way street, you must not be aggressive as you turn. The drivers facing you must turn right or left since they are facing a one-way street with traffic coming towards them. If the drivers facing you are overly aggressive as they turn, you must yield to them. Nobody wins in an accident.

If you are turning left from a one-way street to another one-way street stay on the extreme left side of the street before you turn. Go into the lane which will best suit your next move. If you intend to make a right turn soon, move into the right lane. If you intend to make a left turn soon, move into the extreme left lane. Do not give yourself unnecessary problems. Only experienced, skillful drivers can maneuver into other lanes. Many times drivers cause problems by trying to squeeze into lanes at the last minute. Thoughtful drivers get into the proper lane long before turning.

<u>Turning left on red</u>

Many drivers are unaware that it is permissible to turn left on a red light when going from a one-way street to another one-way street. Of course, you must check traffic coming from the right and allow all pedestrians to go first. You should always pause before executing the left turn on a red light. Do not move if a sign facing you reads "No Turn on Red".

<u>Left turns on green arrows and green lights</u>

Many intersections have left green arrows but there is no sign which reads "left turn signal". In this situation, you can execute a left turn on the green arrow, and you can also do it on the regular green traffic signal when it is safe. You roll out to the center of the intersection and turn when no vehicles are coming towards you.

Some busy intersections have a separate traffic signal and a sign which reads "Left Turn Signal". In this instance you are only permitted to exercise this left turn on the green arrow. This signal usually is hanging in the center of the intersection or it may be on a medial strip in the center of the street. Most of the time there will be an extra lane on the left to make this left turn.

Drivers waiting to make a left turn can not move on the regular green light. They only can go left when the green arrow appears.

Jug handle turns

On some major highways (not turnpikes or expressways), left turns can be extremely dangerous. To ameliorate this potential hazard, "jug Handle Turns" were built into modern highways. Accordingly, when you want to make a left turn and you are confronted with a "Jug Handle", you must stay on the right side of the road. As you approach the intersection, signs will guide you around a circle which will bear to the left directly to the road you wanted. Remember, when you see signs which read "All Left Turns From Right Lane", you know you are approaching a "Jug Handle Turn".

GOING AROUND CIRCLES

When you go around a circle, you must conform to one of the basic tenets of driving which is "STAY IN YOUR LANE". The majority of circles do not have marked lanes. Obviously this makes it more difficult. All circles in this country move counter clockwise. You should yield to all vehicles in the circle before you enter. Your position on the circle depends on where you are going. When you are going to continue on the same route, you would usually drive half way around and then continue on the same route number. Some circles have multiple intersections or side routes. If you are leaving the highway for another road to the right, you should enter the circle to the extreme right. This will give you easy access to the road you want. If you have to go onto another road which is to the left of the one you are on, stay in the middle lane of the circle and work your way over carefully.

No matter which lane you choose, you must stay in it. You cannot swerve from one lane to another in heavy traffic. If you ever find yourself in the wrong lane and you can not leave the circle, it is better to go around the circle again and try to position your vehicle properly. Experienced drivers usually edge their way over when they are in the wrong place sometimes using hand signals.

It is better to practice going around circles in a residential area. As you go around the circle, do not look far away. Look into the center of your lane as it turns. Look down into your lane. Raise your vision slightly as you turn. Go with a friend who drives. Let your friend watch to see if you are staying in the lane. When you feel confident, try a circle which is not too crowded. Do not force yourself if you feel too nervous. If you do not feel ready to try a busy circle, do not do it. Stay within yourself. Realize your limitations. Use sound judgment. Have patience. Do not be goaded by others into doing something that might be hazardous for you.

Many aspiring drivers get overly anxious when turning left at busy intersections. Consequently, they turn the wheel too soon and too much. It is most important to start turning the wheel when you start to pass the center of the intersection. Unless the street you are turning into is less than forty feet wide, you are not to turn the wheel more than two times, right hand first, then left hand. The entire turn will be ruined if you turn the wheel too soon. If you turn too late, you may have to turn the wheel three times. You will notice that the wider the street, the less you turn.

If you are waiting in the middle of the street and can not get through until the traffic signal changes to red, you should be able to move at a speed of eight to ten miles an hour. Be sure that the cars coming towards you have stopped. Do not panic as you turn. The cars will wait for you. Do not push the gas pedal too much.

If this is a problem for you, find a quiet intersection and practice left turns at a speed of ten miles per hour.

When turning left into a narrow street or turning left in a rural area, you may slant your car as you turn as long as you do not interfere with traffic facing you.

CHAPTER 10
REVERSE

Moving backwards is naturally more difficult and confusing as going forward. So it is when reversing in an automobile. New drivers usually need more time to master going back.

Many state examinations require very little reversing so the new driver does not spend enough time learning this important phase of driving.

The new driver must take the extra time to learn reverse. A driver who cannot go back correctly is not a complete driver. If you are not sure of which way to turn the wheel, do not wait until an emergency arises when you are in traffic. In your spare time go to a deserted area and practice.

When moving the lever into "R", it is most important to keep your right foot firmly on the brake pedal. The vehicle should never be moving at this time. It is just as important to keep your right foot firmly on the brake pedal when moving the lever from "R" to "D" or from "D" to "R".

You must remember not to press the gas pedal when changing from "R" to "D" or vice versa. This could cause an accident.

DO NOT LOOK IN MIRROR

Many people look in the mirror when going back. When you look in the mirror, your vision is limited. You can only see what the mirror shows you. You will not see a small child or dog, etc. It may feel uncomfortable to turn your head, but usually you only have to stay in reverse a few seconds.

If you have a problem turning your head because of arthritis or some other medical reason, you will have to use the mirror. Try to turn your head as much as you can and use the mirror sparingly. Go back slowly and keep your right foot near the brake.

Look over your right shoulder when you want to go back straight or when you want to go back towards the right. Look over your left shoulder when you want to go back to your left, but be sure to glance in all directions to see if the street is clear of traffic.

HOW TO PRACTICE REVERSE

1. Find a deserted area.
2. Put lever in "R" with your right foot firmly on the brake.
3. Do not touch the gas pedal if the car rolls by itself.
4. Do not watch the front of the car.
5. Always turn the top of the wheel in the direction you want the back of the car to go.
6. When going back straight, you may place your right arm over the back of the seat. If you have to turn the wheel a lot, use both hands and turn hand over hand.

DO NOT LOOK AT THE FRONT OF THE CAR

You must not look at the front of the car while reversing. Every time you do, you will probably turn the wheel the wrong way. When you look at the front of the car, you automatically will try to straighten out the front. This will cause the back of the car to do the opposite of what you are trying to do. Look at it this way; if you were going forward would you look at the back of the car? Of course not.

The middle-aged new driver usually has more difficulty mastering reverse than the young driver. This does not mean you cannot learn. Doing anything in reverse is usually not easy. Therefore, it is better to proceed slowly and with caution. Never go back unless you are looking behind you. Keep your right foot above the brake while the car is moving.

EXERCISES TO PRACTICE

In reverse, turn the wheel as far as it goes to the left while your foot is on the brake. Now looking over your right shoulder, let the car roll. Turn the wheel to the right until the car starts to go straight back. At this point the car usually will go a little too far to the right so you should turn the wheel back slightly to the left until it is going straight. Do the same exercise, only this time start out in reverse by turning the wheel to the extreme right. Roll back and try to straighten out by turning the wheel to the left.

All new drivers who have problems with this exercise make the same mistake. For example, when they turn the wheel to the extreme right and then turn left to straighten out, the car does not go to the left immediately. At this time, most learners think they are doing something wrong, so they turn the wheel to the right. Of course the car will now be going too far to the right.

New drivers should realize that when the wheel is turned all the way, it must be turned back the other way at least three or four times. If the wheel is turned back slightly, the car will continue to go back in the wrong direction. Keep repeating this exercise until it is understood.

Another good method for practicing reverse is to find an intersection with little or no traffic. Park the car near the corner about two or three feet from the curb. In reverse, try to go back around the corner into the street on the right. Look over your right shoulder and let the car roll back straight until your body approaches the point where the curb turns. Now turn the wheel to the right three or four times. When the car is rolling straight back, turn the wheel to the left about three times. Most beginners turn the wheel to the left too soon. If this happens, the car will move back to the left. Try not to straighten out too soon. Anyone who can perform this exercise successfully understands reverse. This is an excellent way to master reverse and it should be practiced until it is mastered.

Practically every new driver I have taught has made the mistake of forgetting to move the lever to "Drive" after going back in "Reverse".

This is a common mistake. A female learner has just gone back a few feet. Now I say, "Go forward." Instead of changing to "R", she pushes the accelerator. When she realizes her mistake, she reaches for the lever to put it in "D". At the same time the car is still going back because she does not reach for the brake. You must first put your foot on the brake and stop the car. Now you can put the lever on "D" in complete safety. Reaching for the lever, while the car is moving can damage the transmission besides being dangerous.

Nothing confuses new drivers about reverse more than when they are told to always turn the wheel in the opposite direction of where they want the front of the car to go, instead of the way they want the back to go. This method will work when backing out of a parking space or from a driveway. However, suppose you stop at a red light on a fairly narrow street. A large truck in the intersection wants to turn right, but your car is in his turning path. You have to go back. You cannot think of turning opposite to the way you want the front to go since you only want to go back straight. If you really understand reverse, you will look over your right shoulder and if the car does not go back straight, you will know which way to turn the wheel. You will turn the wheel the way you want the back to go.

If the back of the car is going to the left, you will turn the wheel to the right and vice versa. If the car goes back straight, do not turn the wheel. This situation happens to every driver at some time. If it happens to you do not panic. Most of the time the car will roll without touching the accelerator. Look back and let it roll. Only touch the accelerator gently if the car does not move.

Some senior drivers develop a mental block in reverse and it takes them a long time to master it. As I have stated before–practice, practice, practice.

HOW TO TURN AROUND IN A SMALL SPACE

1.   Start out by being about six inches from the curb on the right.

2.   Before starting out check traffic front and rear.

3.   In "D", let the car roll as you turn the wheel completely to the left until you are approximately one foot from the curb. As you are reaching the other side of the street, relax your hands on the wheel so the wheel is not pushed too hard to the left. (If your car does not have power steering, you should start turning the wheel to the right as you are stopping).

4.   Shift into "R" keeping your foot firmly on the brake.

5.   Let the car roll back and turn the wheel all the way to the right at the same time.

6.   Look over your left shoulder behind you to see how close the car is to the curb. Be sure to check traffic in both directions at all times.

7.   As you are stopping, do not turn the wheel too hard as it reaches the end or turn the wheel back slightly to the left.

8.   Shift back to "D", with your foot on the brake, and turn the wheel to the left until the car is turned around facing in the opposite direction.

9.   If the car is still not turned around, repeat the entire operation.

The best method for turning a car around in a small space is to turn the wheel quickly while the car moves slowly.

LEAVING A PARKING SPACE

If you are angle parked in a shopping section, you must go back straight so your car won't scrape a car next to you. Look behind you, left and right, and go back slowly. If your car is not staying straight, turn the wheel in the direction you want the back to go. Try not to oversteer when you make a correction. Watching traffic behind you, back out straight until the front of your car passes the rear tires of the cars next to you. Now turn the wheel in the same direction you want the back of your car to go until the front of your car is facing the way you want to go. If your exit is on your left, you should have turned the wheel to the right when going back or vice versa. As you go back, you should look behind you left and right repeatedly.

FIG. 12 - PARALLEL PARKING

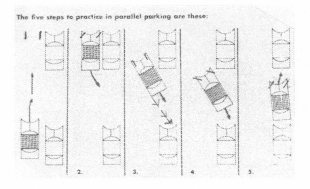

The five steps to practice in parallel parking are these:

LEARNING PARALLEL PARKING

For some unexplainable reason, women seem to have more problems parking than men. Actually parking is not too difficult when it is done systematically. You cannot learn how to parallel park if you do not practice.

In the beginning, select a space that is about six to eight feet larger than the size of your car. As you become more proficient, you can try a smaller space.

Your car should be lined up straight, with the back of your car level with the car alongside of you. There should be approximately two feet of space between your car and the car on your right.

Do not start turning the wheel to the right until your car is moving. Look over your right shoulder. Let your car roll about one foot before turning the wheel. If you start turning the wheel too soon all the way, you may scrape the car at your side when backing in. Be sure the car rolls slowly as you go back. It may be necessary to hold your foot softly on the brake so the car barely moves.

The most critical part of this operation is to know when to turn the wheel back to the left. If you turn back too soon, you will be far from the curb. If you turn too late, you will go up on the curb.

When cars were made so you could see the rear fenders, I would instruct learners to turn the wheel to the left when the rear left fender of your car was pointing to the right headlight of the car behind you. Today you cannot see the rear fenders on most cars. However, as you go back slowly, wait until you can line up the left corner of the rear window on an angle so it is pointing towards the right headlight of the car behind you. Pause and start turning the wheel to the left until you are parked in the space.

Unless you have parked poorly, you can maneuver into your space. If you are in the space, but your right rear tire is on the curb, pull into your space if you have at least three feet of space in front of you. If you are too far from the curb and you have at least three feet in front of you, you can still manage. Turn the wheel to the right three or four times with your foot on the brake. Now let the car roll without gas towards the curb. This exercise should be practiced so you will learn how to go back and forth when necessary.

When you park so poorly that you have no space to maneuver, move out and try again.

REMEMBER THESE THREE RULES

1. Always look back when in reverse;
2. Always turn the top of the wheel in the direction you want the back end to go.
3. Be sure to move slowly. Do not touch accelerator if vehicle is moving. Keep your foot above the brake.

Almost everyone can learn to parallel park with enough practice. However, if you have a problem turning your head, look for a space large enough so you can enter it going forward.

HOW TO PARK GOING FORWARD

1. Put on the right turn signal at least half a block before the parking space.
2. Check the rear mirror. If a car is behind you, wave the driver on with your left hand.
3. Slow down to ten miles an hour when you are approximately twenty yards from the parking space. Do not stop.
4. Drive into the parking space between five and ten miles per hour.

5. Pull into the space looking at the center of the parked car in front of you. This will help you park straight.

6. If you are too close to the car in front, go back a few feet. Be sure to look behind you and if the car is not straight turn the wheel the same way you want the back to go.

7. Pick a space that is at least as large as the length of three cars.

CHAPTER 11
REVIEW OF THE INSTRUMENT PANEL

Most Common Questions Asked by New Drivers

All drivers should know how to read and become familiar with the instrument panel, gauges and controls of the automobile. There are slight differences in some automobiles. Some of them have some indicators which others do not have. These are the most common:

1.<u>Speedometer</u> -

This indicates the miles per hour at which the car travels. Some cars show a red line or mark at the fifty-five mile per hour point, which is the maximum speed allowed on most roads in the United States.

2.<u>Odometer</u> -

The odometer measures the number of miles the car has been driven. Many vehicles have a separate trip odometer that you can set to zero at the beginning of the trip.

3.<u>Fuel Gauge</u> -

This shows the amount of gasoline in the fuel tank. It is a good policy to keep the fuel supply reasonably full whenever possible. In cold weather a low fuel tank promotes condensation. The water may freeze and stop the flow of fuel to the engine.

4.<u>Temperature Gauge</u> -

Some vehicles do not have a temperature gauge. In these vehicles a red light will appear on the instrument panel when the car overheats. If this happens, stop immediately. Driving with this condition can seriously damage your engine. If you do have a temperature gauge stop if the indicator on the gauge is nearing the red warning mark. Sometimes the engine will overheat if you are moving very slowly on a hot day with the air conditioner running. You can cool the engine if you allow the engine to idle in "P" or "N" for a few minutes. You can also press the accelerator gently at the same time. Do not run the air conditioner while you are doing this. If there is nothing wrong with your vehicle, the temperature should come down. When this happens, you can turn the air conditioner on provided you can drive at least twenty-five miles per hour. New automobiles seldom overheat, but it may happen if your vehicle has a faulty cooling system.

5.Oil Pressure Gauge -

The oil pressure gauge warns you whenever oil is not circulating properly in the engine. If the red oil light comes on while the motor is running, shut off the engine. Driving without enough oil can cause irreversible damage to the engine. However, if the engine stalls and the red oil light appears, this does not mean that the oil supply is low. When you restart the engine, the oil light will not appear.

6.Alternator Gauge -

The alternator produces the electricity that powers the electrical system of the car. If electricity is not produced as fast as it is used, it is drained from the battery. If your vehicle has an indicator, the needle should be above the center of the gauge most of the time. When electricity is not produced as fast as it is used, the engine will eventually stop running. In many cars a warning light is used in place of the alternator gauge. When this light appears, have your vehicle checked by a mechanic.

7.Gear Selector Lever -

The gear selector lever controls the connection between the engine and the wheels. This lever is attached to the transmission. In some vehicles, the lever is located on the right side of the steering column. In others, it is mounted on the floor to the right of the driver.

Know your vehicle

Everyone who drives a car should be familiar with all of the controls. Before driving you should know how to use the heater, air conditioner, wipers and washer, lights, defroster, etc. Know how to adjust the fan lever when using the air conditioner, defroster and heater. You should know how to adjust your seat and know how to release the hood.

<u>Check Brake Light</u>

If you forget to release the parking brake, a red light will appear on the instrument panel. Be sure to release the parking brake if this happens.

<u>QUESTIONS MOST NEW OR MIDDLE-AGED DRIVERS ASK</u>

Q.I would like to drive, but I think I am too nervous. Can I overcome this feeling?

A.Nervousness by itself will not stop you from driving. Practically every new driver is nervous. Some are more nervous than others. As you drive your nervousness should disappear almost entirely.

Q.(Same person) Will my nervousness ever go away completely?

A.Probably not. You may always be slightly nervous. However, it is better to be slightly nervous when driving. You will be more careful. A completely relaxed person may be careless behind the wheel.

Q.I have poor hearing. Can I still drive safely?

A.Yes. Poor hearing will not stop you. As you drive, you will have to make an effort to use your eyes and mirrors more than the average driver.

Q.When should I start using the brake?

A.This question is asked very frequently by neophyte drivers. There is no certain time to use the brake. The momentum of the car determines when to start using the brake. The faster the car is moving, the sooner you apply the brake. If you are going on a downgrade, you use the brake sooner. If you are going uphill, you use the brake later. It is better to use the brake sooner than later. If you use the brake too soon, it is easy to take your foot off the brake and touch the accelerator. If you use the brake too late, you will probably press the brake too hard and the car will not stop smoothly. With enough experience, you will learn how and when to use the brake.

Q.If two cars have an accident at an intersection, is the driver who had the stop sign solely responsible?

A.This is not necessarily so. In an intersection, usually both parties are responsible. When one car goes through a stop sign, the other driver should be able to stop if he or she is driving defensively. If the driver who does not have a stop sign is exceeding the speed limit, the accident will be partially his fault. There are extenuating circumstances in many accidents and all the facts have to be considered before a decision is reached.

Q.Who has the right of way at an unprotected intersection? Consider both streets as equal.

A. Right of way does not really exist. You must never think you have the right of way. Both vehicles enter the intersection at the same time, the car on the left should yield to the one on the right. However, if the car on the left arrives at the intersection first and is already crossing the street, then the car on the right should yield.

Q.This is probably the most asked question–When I have to make a turn, do I use the brake or the gas?

A.This depends on the speed in which you are approaching the intersection. If you are moving more than ten miles per hour, use the brake. If you are driving between five and ten miles per hour, do not press the accelerator harder. When going downhill around a curve, use the brake. When starting to turn at a stopped position, all new drivers should not touch the gas pedal. Let the car roll by itself unless it does not move. If the car stops while turning, take your foot away from the brake so the car can roll.

Q.What do I do if a tire has a blowout?

A.If a rear tire blows out, the back end of the car will sway. If the right front tire blows out, the car will swerve to the right. If it is the left front tire, the car swerves to the left.

If you have a blowout do not press the brake immediately. Grip the steering wheel hard and try to keep the car straight. When the car is under control, apply the brake gently and try to pull over to the side.

If you have good tires, you probably will never have a blowout. The most dangerous blowouts occur at excessive speeds.

Q.(Stick shift) Sometimes when I want to shift from neutral to first gear, the lever seems to stick. What should I do?

A.With the lever in neutral, take your foot away from the clutch. Now depress the clutch again and try to shift into first gear again. If it still seems stuck repeat the process.

Q.To stay in my lane should I look down at the line on the left or should I watch the line on my right?

A.Neither one is correct. You should aim high with your vision and look in the middle of the lane. Your eyes should be scanning up and down constantly. Never stare while you are driving. However, on a narrow country road, try to stay near the middle of the road, especially when cars are coming towards you. Otherwise you may veer too far to the right.

Q.A school bus approaches from the opposite direction with the upper red lights flashing. It stops. Do I have to stop?

A.Yes. Children will be getting off the bus. You must stop at least ten feet away. You do not proceed until the red lights stop flashing, and the children are off the street. You must wait even if the traffic signal is green. You do not proceed until the red lights stop flashing, and the children are off the street. It does not matter where the school bus is. You do not move if the top lights of the bus are flashing or if children are still on the street.

THE FOLLOWING STATEMENTS ARE TRUE AND FALSE.

When approaching a crest of a hill, you should keep to the extreme right.True

Pedestrians should always walk on the right side of the road.False.

Older people have the same reaction time as younger people.False

You must have your operator's license with you when operating a motor vehicle.True

When entering a highway from a private driveway or from a public driveway, you should yield to all traffic.True.

Impatience on the part of motorists contribute to many accidents.True.

Worn tires reduce traction.True.

When you drive over the crest of a hill, the pull of gravity makes the car go faster. True.

When parking your car on a downgrade, always turn your front wheels to the right. True.

There are more accidents in dry weather than rainy weather.False.

Normal reaction time is three fourths of a second.True.

Tires will be more likely to overheat when they are over inflated.True.

A small amount of alcohol will not affect your driving.False.

Most accidents are due to mechanical failure.False.

If you are driving at forty miles per hour, it will take you sixty feet to stop.False

(150 feet to stop)

After driving through water, your brakes get wet. Continue to drive slowly and pump the brakes lightly until they dry out.True.

When you are making a right or left turn on a green light, you must yield to all pedestrians. True

COMMON DRIVING EMERGENCIES

Q.You are driving at night on a straight road. A vehicle comes towards you with high beam lights shining in your eyes. You switch the brights on and off, but the other driver does not lower the high beam.

Answer - Do not look at the lights of the car. Drive slowly. Pump your brake lightly to warn the driver behind you. Look at the right side of your lane and try to stay close to it as the car passes you.

Q.You are on your side of a two-lane highway. A car comes towards you partially in your lane. You swerve to the right. Your right front wheel goes on the shoulder.

Answer - Do not try to swerve back into your lane. Ease up on the accelerator. Keep a firm grip on the wheel. Pump the brake lightly. When your car slows down, go back in your lane gradually.

Q.You are driving on an icy road. You touch your brake and hit an icy patch. The rear of the car skids to the right.

Answer - Do not step on the brake. Turn the steering wheel to the right. When you feel you have control, pump the brake very lightly.

Q.You are driving on a two-lane highway. Ahead of you on the right side, a boy on a bicycle swerves towards you. Your left side is clear.

<u>Answer</u> - Blow your horn immediately and steer to the left.

NOMENCLATURE YOU SHOULD KNOW

<u>Acceleration Lane</u> - A special traffic lane that permits vehicles entering a highway to gain speed before merging with fast moving vehicles already on the highway.

<u>Access Ramp</u> - A turning roadway at an interchange that permits traffic to move from one highway to another on a different level.

<u>Carbon Monoxide</u>- A poisonous, colorless, odorless and tasteless gas.

<u>Field of Vision</u> - The actual area of range a person can see in front within an arc of one hundred and eighty degrees.

<u>Peripheral Vision</u> - The ability to see to the sides while looking straight ahead.

<u>Tunnel Vision</u> - When a person has a narrow field of vision and cannot see to the sides while looking straight ahead.

<u>Median</u> - Non traveled strip or area separating traffic moving in the opposite direction.

<u>Divided Highway</u> - One with a center or medial strip built into the highway separating it into one-way roads (a physical barrier).

<u>Overtake</u> - To catch up with another vehicle.

<u>Certificate Of Title</u> - When you own a motor vehicle, you must have this.

<u>Revocation</u> - Cancellation of the privilege of driving.

<u>Safe Following Distance</u> - At least a car length for each ten miles per hour of speed.

Competition - What is desirable in athletic contests, but dangerous for a motorist.

Blind Spot - An area outside a car not visible to the driver even with the aid of mirrors.

CHAPTER 12
ACCIDENT FREE DRIVING

There are four very important rules for safe driving. They are as follows:

1.Stay in your Lane

When you are driving on a boulevard or multi-lane highway, you must never, never stare at passing vehicles. This could be extremely hazardous to your health. Staring at passing vehicles on either side of you gives you the illusion that they are running into you. An inexperienced driver could turn the wheel abruptly in the opposite direction and strike a vehicle in the other lane. The bottom line is what I have been emphasizing all through this book. Look straight ahead and you will stay in your lane. Stay in your lane whether you are in traffic or if you are alone on the road. Do not change your lane unless it is necessary, but be sure to check the rear before you do.

2.Check Traffic before changing Lanes

Never ever change lanes unless you are positive you can do so without interfering with another driver. Before looking in either mirror, set your position on the road so you will not swerve. Do not move the wheel while looking in the mirror. When you can see that the car will stay in the lane for the next five or ten seconds, look in the rear mirror for one second. Now look in front of you to observe the traffic scene and to see if you are staying in your lane. To move over to the left, look in the left side mirror for one second. Again look in front of you to check traffic. Remember you must never stare in the mirror for more than one second at a time. Take quick one second glances and look ahead in between glances. To drive a car safely, you must always take quick glances when you are looking away from the road in front of you.

When it is safe to move over to the lane on your left, put on your left signal and look about twenty yards away into the center of the lane you are entering. If another car is there, look towards the center of it. When you change lanes do not use the brake. This could be dangerous. Maintain your speed. When you change lanes there should be no car behind you on your left. Look twice before you make your move. Do not forget to take off your turn signal after you are in the lane.

Moving over to the lane on the right could be more difficult because of the blind spot on the right side . Of course, you must look in the rear mirror following the same procedure as explained for going into the left lane. Glance, do not stare. Before moving over to the right, you must turn your head quickly over your right shoulder to see if a car is on your right side. Again be sure to signal before moving over and do not brake while doing so. Do not move to the right lane until no car is in the right lane behind you. Remember this very important rule–NEVER, EVER MOVE THE WHEEL TO THE LEFT OR TO THE RIGHT WITHOUT LOOKING BEHIND YOU. Many an accident happens when a drive absent mindedly turns the wheel without checking the rear.

3.<u>Do Not Stare at Distractions</u>

Many inexperienced drivers have a tendency to have "sticky" eyes when a distraction appears. Remember, never to take your vision away from the driving path in front of you for more than a second at a time. You must learn to take quick glances at any distraction, but your eyes must always go back to the road in front of you. If something unusual is happening in front of you, put your foot above the brake pedal. Look in the mirror quickly. Do not jam the brake suddenly. The best drivers know how to glance quickly without staring. Almost every rear end collision is caused when the driver in the rear takes his eyes away from the road too long. A rear end collision could also possibly occur if anyone suddenly jams the brake. Rear end collisions in most instances are avoidable–yet it is probably the most prevalent of all accidents.

4.Proper Use of the Horn

Using the horn at the right time can prevent accidents. The horn should be used whenever you think another driver, who should see you, is not looking in your direction. For example, you are about to enter an intersection. You do not have a stop sign, but the intersecting street has a stop sign. The driver at the stop sign is starting to cross the street, but he is looking to the left only and you are crossing on his right. "Blow" the horn immediately, but keep your foot over the brake so you can stop if necessary.

Sometimes drivers making left turns forget to look to the right. If this driver is violating your space and does not look towards you, "Blow" the horn–let him know you are there. Of course, your foot should be on the brake at the same time, but do not stop suddenly.

Always be on the lookout for drivers pulling out of parking spaces in front of you. Do not assume that the driver sees you. If he is not looking towards you, "Blow" the horn. Do not stare at the other car. Glance quickly at it with your foot touching your brake. If the other driver does not see you, he will stop as soon as he hears the horn. If the driver does not hear you because his windows are closed, do not jam your brake. Try to stop gently, but do not turn your wheel sharply to the left. You should have observed if a car is behind you. If so, you should put your left hand out the window to warn the drivers behind you.

If another driver is going backwards towards you, you must sound the horn. Stopping your car will not help if the other driver does not know you are there.

USE YOUR OWN JUDGEMENT

It is important not to always do what other drivers want you to do. For example, you are approaching a busy intersection. The signal light is green and you want to make a left turn. A driver coming towards you also wants to make a left turn. He wants to be kind to you so he motions to you to make your left turn. Cars are streaming behind him and are coming towards you. The drivers passing him have no intention of letting you make your left turn. In fact, they do not even know he is motioning for you to turn. If you listen to this man, you could cause a major accident. Disregard this man and wait for all traffic to clear before turning. This man means well, but he is not thinking clearly. In a situation like this, if multiple lanes of traffic are coming towards you, you must wait for all lanes to be free of oncoming traffic.

Conversely, do not motion for another driver facing you to make a left turn at an intersection when cars are behind you or beside you. This could also cause a serious accident. Do not be a traffic director. The driver facing you should make the left turn when his way is clear.

Shopping Center Hazards

Driving through shopping centers can be very hazardous if you are not careful. When you are driving between parked cars on both sides, be wary of drivers going in reverse towards you. Drive very slowly and honk the horn at the slightest movement of a car going back towards you. Conversely, if you are going back out of a parking space, look behind you left and right before moving out. Do not touch the gas pedal if the car rolls slowly by itself.

Use Horn for Pedestrians and Children

Another instance to use the horn is to warn pedestrians when they do not see you. If a pedestrian is walking ahead of you, let him know you are behind him. Tap the horn gently. Do the same if children are playing on the street. Use the horn on small streets if children are playing on the pavement–especially when there are lots of parked cars. Children can run into the street suddenly. Hold your foot near the brake pedal and do not drive more than ten miles an hour. Someday, you may be glad you did, if a child ever darts in front of you.

Check Rear before changing Lanes

Do not think you can change your lane just because you put on your turn signal. Put on your turn signal only when it is safe to change lanes. You can cause a serious accident by not waiting until you can change lanes without interfering with the flow of traffic. Other drivers cannot get out of your way just because your signal is on. Use common sense.

When there is a constant flow of traffic behind you and you see an opening to pass, do not use your brake. Slowing down when changing lanes can trigger a traffic accident. If you are not sure of changing the lane quickly, then do not. Wait until the traffic behind you becomes lighter. With more experience you should be able to execute lane changes quickly and safely.

Passing double parked Vehicles

Do not feel trapped when a double parked vehicle looms in front of you, especially on a busy street. Everyone is moving, so the inexperienced driver gets the notion that it would be wrong to stop. It is safe to stop and wait. Remember that all drivers behind you see the double parked vehicle. Consequently, they will not run into you. Usually the drivers behind you are impatient so they will pass you. When you stop, leave at least one car length between you and the double parked vehicle so you will have enough space to pull out. However, you are not to move to your left until the way is clear. Put on the left turn signal and steer away from the parked vehicle. Do not stare at it. Be careful not to pull back into the right lane too soon. Pass it by at least ten yards before pulling back into the right lane.

THE PROBLEM OF CHANGING LIGHTS

A new driver is often confused when confronted with changing traffic lights. Some new drivers hope the traffic signal changes to red long before they reach the intersection so they will not have a problem.

When a signal light has been green for a long time, you should slow down so you can stop smoothly if the signal changes to red. Many drivers do the opposite. When they encounter a "stale" green light, they drive faster and many times go through red lights. They have already made the decision to go and a red traffic signal will not stop them. For this reason, it is wise for a driver crossing this intersection to check traffic carefully soon after a red light changes to green. In city traffic it is obvious that most accidents happen at intersections.

Do not ever stop at a light changing to red if you have to jam the brake. You could be struck in the rear. Always glance in the rear mirror as you are stopping. If you see the car behind you is going fast, it may be better to cross over.

Making the right decision is important. Every time you get behind the wheel, you will have to make decisions. The faster you drive, the quicker your decision will have to be made.

When driving on the highway and the light is changing to red it is better not to stop if you are driving more than forty miles an hour, unless you have plenty of time and space to stop. In city traffic it is easier to make a decision because you will be driving at a slower speed. If you can stop without jamming the brake, it is advisable to do so. When in doubt it is better to stop as long as you are not moving too fast.

<u>Flashing Signal Lights</u>

There are people driving today who do not know what to do when confronted with a flashing red or yellow traffic signal. When you come to an intersection with a flashing red light, you should stop and proceed when the way is clear on the left and right. The drivers coming from the left or right usually have a flashing yellow signal. They do not have to stop. When you have a flashing yellow signal, you are to proceed with caution.

<u>Railroad Crossings</u>

A flashing red signal at a railroad crossing is different. You stop and wait for the red signal to stop flashing. You proceed when the gate opens. Never stop on the tracks. If you cannot drive past the tracks, do not move. Wait until you can continue driving away from the tracks.

Most railroad crossings are not controlled. These have a Crossbuck which is a large white X-shaped sign or a yellow warning sign. There are no gates or flashers. Be extra careful. Be sure your windows are open so you can hear the train. Check both sides of the tracks if there are two sets of tracks.

<u>How to avoid Accidents when crossing intersections on Green Lights</u>

If you drive long enough, the time may come when someone will go through a red light at the same instant that you are approaching the intersection. There is something you can do about this precarious situation.

Every time you come to an intersection with a green light, take your foot away from the accelerator and place it above the brake pedal. Do not press the brake, but have your foot ready. If you observe a car going through the red light, touch the horn and use the brake. Do not jam the brake unless absolutely necessary. If you are alert, you will know if a car is too close to your rear. Putting your hand out will help to warn the driver behind you.

Most drivers do not bother to follow the procedure just explained. Instead they accelerate at intersections with green lights.

This simple habit can save your life or prevent you or others from serious injury. Using this method at intersections goes beyond defensive driving. It is super defensive driving. Do it. Someday you will be glad you did. Do not forget to glance quickly to your left and right as you approach the intersection.

LOOK AHEAD

Your eyes should be constantly scanning the traffic scene ahead of you, behind you, and to your sides. Take quick glances. Never stare.

If the car or cars in front of you are braking for no apparent reason, (their brake lights are on) try to ascertain why they are slowing down. At the same time, pump your brake pedal gently a few times so the drivers behind you will notice your flashing brake lights. Slow down until the congestion has cleared.

YOUR EYES AND BRAIN WORK TOGETHER. YOUR BRAIN TELLS YOU WHAT TO DO AFTER GETTING THE INFORMATION FROM YOUR EYES. IF YOUR EYES LOOK IN THE WRONG PLACE, YOUR BRAIN WILL RECEIVE THE WRONG MESSAGE FROM YOUR EYES. CONSEQUENTLY

YOU COULD STEER INCORRECTLY OR BRAKE AT THE WRONG TIME AND CAUSE AN ACCIDENT.

When driving, you must not let your mind wander. Concentrate only on your driving problems so your eyes and your brain can work together in coordination as a team. Give your brain the right message and your hands will guide you correctly.

ANTICIPATING PROBLEMS

An intelligent, skillful driver must be aware of impending traffic problems before they happen. Aggressive drivers do not allow for the mistakes of others. The aggressive driver has no patience. In many situations, skill will not compensate for aggressive driving. Lack of patience by many drivers is the cause of many automobile tragedies.

A knowledgeable driver should be able to sense what another driver is about to do. Assume you are driving on a busy boulevard. A vehicle on your left is crowding the vehicle in front of it. This driver is moving aggressively, but the driver in front of him is impeding his progress. It is obvious that this aggressive driver is looking for a way to pass. At this point, you should realize that this aggressive driver may try to pass by moving in front of you. Check the traffic behind you and tap your brake lightly to warn the driver behind you that you are slowing down. As soon as the aggressive driver sees you leave a space, he will move in front of you and pass. When driving on boulevards or highways this situation will happen frequently. Be ready for it.

DRIVING IN SNOW, RAIN AND AT NIGHT

Many people avoid driving in the snow, but sometimes it is necessary. Other times it may start snowing while you are driving. If possible, try to avoid driving while it is snowing. Besides the hazard of slippery roads, poor visibility front and rear could pose a serious problem.

The best vehicle in the snow is, of course, a four wheel drive vehicle, especially a four wheel drive sport utility vehicle. These vehicles will do better in deep snow or deep water as they are built higher from the ground.

Equip your car with good snow tires. If you have a front wheel drive car, put the snow tires on the front wheels. A good idea is to put all season mud and snow tires on all four wheels. Under no conditions should you drive in the snow with worn out tires. This is asking for trouble. If you drive carefully and with intelligence, you will be able to drive in the snow. However, there are certain times when no one should be driving. When the streets are unusually icy, stay where you are and do not drive.

If you are driving a rear wheel drive car, load your trunk with approximately two hundred pounds of weights. This will give you better traction in the snow or rain. Before driving in the snow, be sure to have a full gas tank so your fuel line will not freeze. Also, fill the windshield washer reservoir. If your exhaust pipe is immersed in snow, be sure to clear it out before driving. This could cause carbon monoxide to escape into the car possibly causing serious health problems or death. When planning a trip in snowy terrain, take along a small shovel, a flashlight, rock salt sand or ashes.

To help you drive safely in snow and ice, you should drive slowly and brake gently. Allow plenty of space between you and the car in front of you. To avoid a loss of traction, a driver must know how to ease up on the brake before it locks. Practice braking on an empty lot to test your brakes and improve your skill. Pressing too hard on the gas pedal especially from a stopped position can also cause loss of traction.

If you skid, the slower you are driving, the less you will skid. Take your foot away from the brake. If you panic and jam the brake, the skid will worsen. When the car skids, the tires are sliding. The idea is to get them to start revolving, so you can steer the car.

Your car will not skid as easily on soft fluffy snow. It will skid more when the sun puts a glaze on the ice. When you drive slowly on ice and do not press the brake hard, you will not skid as much. However, if you are caught in bad weather and your car skids, do not panic. Always turn the wheel in the direction of your skid. For example, if the back of the car starts to slide towards the right, turn the wheel to the right. If the back of the car starts to slide towards the left, turn the wheel to the left. If you are driving slowly, you will be able to stop safely. Skidding is dangerous when the car is moving too fast and you press the brake too hard.

If you are starting out on ice and your wheels keep spinning, do not press hard on the gas pedal. You can burn out the transmission. If the car does not move forward try to move back in "R". Move the wheel so you can get the tires on a different track. Try moving back and forth until you get out. However, if you are still stuck on the ice, put sand, chains or any substance to melt the ice under the tires. What you **should not do** is to put the car in first gear (low gear).

Low gear will increase the tendency of the wheels to spin, especially on slippery surfaces like ice, snow, and rain-covered roads. In fact, if you have a manual transmission, start out in second or third gear to help get the car moving and to minimize the tendency of the wheels to spin.

When driving on an icy street and you know you have to stop at the intersection, try to use the brake on the least icy section of the street. If you are turning in the snow, use the brake gently before you make the turn. Always look in the center of the lane as you turn. This follows that hard and fast rule I advocate strongly-"Look Where you Want to Go."

Do not pump the brake if your car has anti-lock brakes. Simply press the brake and hold it. The ABS system will do the pumping for you. If you do not have anti-lock brakes, pump gingerly.

If you are ever driving on an icy road there is something you can do that might help. Usually the car skids when the brake is pushed too hard, but sometimes if the ice is very slippery you may skid slightly even though you apply gentle pressure. When you see a stop sign or a red signal light, put your indicator lever in neutral ("N") about ten or fifteen feet before you stop. In "N" the engine is disengaged from the transmission and the car can be stopped easier since the engine is not pulling the car. When you are ready to go simply put the lever back in "D" and start out slowly.

DRIVING IN THE RAIN

Every time it rains, the accident rate increases because people continue to drive as if the ground were dry. I do not think that most older drivers are guilty of driving too fast on wet roads. Speeding over puddles of water causes the car to hydroplane. When this happens, the car skims on the water and the steering and braking become ineffective. Driving on gravel and mud could also be hazardous. Drive slowly and do not jam the brake pedal under these conditions.

Although driving in the rain is less hazardous than driving in the snow, the rules are similar. You will not skid as easily as you would in the snow, but you should use the brake pedal gingerly. If you press hard on the accelerator from a standing still position, your wheels may spin.

Be careful at the beginning of a rainfall. The rain activates the dry oil on the ground making it slippery. Be sure to leave extra space between you and the car in front. Do not brake hard and do start out slowly

Good visibility is especially important in inclement weather. If your defroster is not doing the job, turn on the air conditioner. This will clear all of your windows. When driving in the daytime during heavy rain, put on your low beam headlights.

SPACE CUSHION

Never tailgate. Try to keep a safe following distance from the car in front. If the driver in front of you stops suddenly, you may not be able to stop in time. Tailgating interferes with the field of vision in front of you. At a speed of thirty miles per hour, stay three cars away from the car in front of you. At forty miles an hour, stay about four cars away. In bad weather increase your following distance. If a driver is tailgating you, let him pass you. When a car stops in front of you, stop at least a half car length away.

You should also try to have a space cushion on both sides of you. If possible try to avoid being side by side with other cars so you could swerve to avoid an accident.

REACTION TIME

The time it takes to make a decision and move your foot from the gas pedal to the brake pedal is called reaction time. Normal reaction time is about three fourths of a second. As we get older our reaction time may get longer. That is another reason why senior drivers should not drive too fast. The faster you drive, the less time you have to think and act. Do not allow horn blowers to upset you and change your driving. As you improve, you will be able to drive faster and keep the car under your control. In a thirty-five mile per hour speed limit most drivers exceed the speed limit. There is nothing wrong with going twenty-five miles per hour if you feel comfortable. Remember that if you go too fast and have an accident, you may be held responsible.

NIGHT DRIVING

Many older people can not see too well at night. Have your eyes checked if you are having problems seeing at night. Do not drive at night unless your eyes can penetrate the darkness.

At twilight put on your low beam lights and keep them on. Low beam lights are usually used at night. High beam lights are to be used only on extremely dark roads when no cars are coming towards you. If a car is coming towards you for less than five hundred feet, switch back to low beam lights. It is unlawful to use high beam lights in a city or town. High beams could blind the driver coming towards you.

It is more difficult to drive at night than it is to drive during the daylight hours. When it is raining at night the problem is compounded because of the glare from the wet streets. If a car is coming towards you with high beam lights, glance towards the right edge of your lane. Do not look at the headlights of the other car. When driving on a foggy day or night, always use the low beams.

Driving at night is much more tiring than driving during the day. If you go on a trip at night, plan to stop and rest your eyes. Here are some important rules for night time driving.

1. Be sure your windshield is clean.
2. Slow down.
3. Avoid glare. Do not look at headlights.
4. Increase following distance.
5. Use lights properly.

WATCH FOR PEDESTRIANS

Almost half of all pedestrians killed or injured in traffic are struck down at night. The problem is compounded when the pedestrians are wearing dark clothing; especially in the rain.

The worst pedestrians are usually those who do not drive. A person who does not drive usually has no idea of the poor visibility situations. People who drive should be more careful pedestrians than those who do not drive.

COLOR VISION PROBLEMS

Color blindness is a trait inherent more in men than women. The top traffic light is always red, the middle light is always yellow, and the bottom light is always green.

Peripheral Vision

This is the ability to see to the sides, while looking straight ahead. Some people's field of vision is better than others. Most people have a field of vision of approximately one hundred and eighty degrees. This means their peripheral vision is ninety degrees on each side. A driver's peripheral vision should be at least one hundred and forty degrees.

Tunnel Vision

Some people can only see straight ahead. They have very little or no side vision at all. These people are at a great disadvantage when driving. People with tunnel vision or below average peripheral vision should reduce speed at points where anything could be approaching from the sides. It is necessary for these people to turn their heads more at intersections or points of merging traffic. If you have tunnel vision or poor peripheral vision, let an ophthalmologist advise you about driving.

Know the Traffic Scene Around You

If there is nothing wrong with your eyes, do not drive as if you are in a tunnel. Your peripheral vision should pick up any movement on your sides. You cannot drive safely for too long if you are oblivious to the cars behind you and on your left and right side. However, you should not stare in the mirror. Quick glances in the mirror are best. Sometimes a quick turn of your head, especially to the right is helpful. The best way to see a car over your right shoulder is to turn your head quickly. Be sure not to turn the wheel when taking your quick glances. By knowing what the traffic scene is around you, you will know if you have an escape route in an emergency.

If something happens on your left and you know the right side is clear, turn to the right. A new middle-aged driver may not be proficient enough to do this at the beginning, but with practice, the new driver will improve. Driving can be compared to typing or playing a musical instrument. The more you practice, the better you will be. Determination and perseverance will prevail.

Everyone who drives has to know their own capabilities. The best time to learn how to drive is when you are young. At this time in your life, you are not nervous, your coordination and learning ability are excellent. In today's world, older people are in better physical condition than ever before. Therefore, learning how to drive after sixty is not unusual. However, not every senior citizen can drive a car everywhere.

MOST ACCIDENTS ARE CAUSED BY

1.   Drivers under the influence of alcohol or drugs.
2.   Excessive speed.
3.   Impatient drivers.
4.   Staring at distractions.

Many inexperienced drivers have a tendency to have "sticky" eyes when confronted with a distraction. Remember to never take your eyes away from the road for more than one second. You must learn to take quick glances at any distraction, but your vision must always go back to the road in front of you. If something is happening in front of you, put your foot above the brake. Look in the mirror for one second. Do not jam the brake suddenly for no real reason. The best drivers know how to glance quickly without staring. Almost every rear end collision is caused by the driver in the rear taking his eyes away from the road too long. Rear end collisions would almost never happen if drivers would pay attention to the road. Yet it is one of the most common of all accidents.

Drive with patience

Impatient drivers cause many accidents. They are constantly trying to pass everyone in front of them. Impatient drivers usually are guilty of driving too fast. To be a safe driver, you must drive with patience. Middle aged drivers have good driving records because most of them observe this very important rule. At least forty percent of all teenagers and those under twenty-five are involved in serious accidents. This reason is obvious. They are impatient and they drive too fast.

If Your Brakes Fail

If you keep your car in good condition and have the car inspected regularly, you should not have any brake failure. However, if by some rare occurrence, your brake pedal goes down to the floor and you are driving faster than twenty miles per hour, pump the brake quickly a few times. If the brake does not work shift your lever into low gear. This will slow you down. If necessary use the emergency brake (slowly). Try to pull over to the side and put on your hazard lights until help arrives. Never stop the car by putting the indicator on "P" while the car is moving unless you are willing to break the transmission.

Red Lights and Stop Signs

Why do some drivers have a tendency to drive through a red signal light or stop sign? One obvious reason is lack of concentration. Some people have a natural inclination to daydream. Their daydreaming is not only confined to driving. There is no place for lack of concentration behind the wheel. Accidents will surely follow.

As I have reiterated many times, improper use of your vision can lead to traffic accidents. Driving through city

124

streets, you must know what is going on at every intersection. Do not stare two or three blocks away. Do not continuously stare straight ahead. You are not in a tunnel.

When you are approximately one hundred feet from an intersection start glancing quickly to the left and right to see if the way is clear. Before glancing left and right you should already know if you have a red light or a stop sign. At the same time you should be staying in your lane by not moving the wheel while you are glancing at the intersection. If you have a green signal light, do not press the accelerator as you approach the intersection. Place you right foot above the brake pedal without pressing on it. Glance quickly left and right as you approach the intersection. If another car is going through the red light, you will be able to stop.

When approaching an intersection with a stop sign, glance quickly to your left to look for a four - way stop sign. As you get more exposure to driving, you will become more proficient in the foregoing procedures.

STAYING FOCUSED

The fundamental driving problem for older people is the inability to stay focused. Seniors have a short attention span, lose concentration, and become distracted too easily.

When driving to a strange destination, be sure you know how to get there. If other people are in the vehicle, do not engage in conversation with them. Pay attention to the traffic scene. If possible have a person who drives sit beside you to help you observe traffic conditions. Be alert and try to relax.

When driving alone, do not let your mind wander. Concentrate on your driving. Pay attention to stop signs and traffic signals. Drive in the right lane so other drivers can pass you safely. Many seniors are apprehensive about making left turns in traffic. If you stay awake at night worrying about left turns, there is usually a way to avoid it. Usually you can pass the busy intersection and make right turns to get back to the street you need.

As we get older reaction time becomes slower and our vision worsens. Therefore, our concentration should be greater to compensate for our failings. If you feel uneasy driving more than forty miles an hour, stay away from expressways, and limited access highways. There are usually other roads which lead to your destination.

Drive at night only after checking with an ophthalmologist. Never drive under the influence of alcohol. Do not drive after taking medication that makes you drowsy. If your driving becomes erratic and inconsistent, your family or friends will tell you. That is the time to discontinue driving. However, if your health and vision are satisfactory, you should be able to drive up to a ripe old age.

"I have great extra-sensory perception for this sort of thing."

Cartoon C: Unsafe to Pass

CHAPTER 13
REAR END COLLISIONS

Rear end collisions are the most prevalent and most preventable of all types of vehicle accidents. The greatest obstacle to resolving these world-wide disasters is the human species. At the top of the list is the drunken driver, male or female, who destroys his/her own life besides killing or maiming innocent victims. Unfortunately, rear end collisions are an affliction without a foreseeable solution.

Inexplicably, truck drivers are responsible for many rear end crashes with the most calamitous results. Truck drivers have demolished motionless automobiles, in broad daylight on state turnpikes and highways. Many truck drivers speed to make more deliveries, and do not get enough sleep or rest. Young people, who inflict rear end collisions on unsuspecting victims, are usually guilty of excessive speed, impatience, and inattention, especially when distracted by other teenagers in the vehicle. Imbibing alcoholic liquids is also a factor.

Everyday drivers commit mayhem on the highways because they momentarily look away from the traffic scene in front of them. People who have been driving for many years sometimes tend to become complacent or careless.

There is a stigma attached to a senior citizen if he or she is the perpetrator in a rear end collision. The popular opinion of most people is that older people should not drive. As people get older, reaction time becomes slower and their vision worsens. Accordingly, it is incumbent for them to be focused at all times to compensate for their shortcomings.

When waiting for a red signal light to change, there is almost nothing a driver can do except to glance in the rear view mirror. If you see a vehicle approaching your rear too fast, quickly put on the hazard lights and sound the horn loudly. If possible move over to another lane. Be sure your seat belt is attached and pray.

Alcoholism is a human frailty. Rear end collisions will continue unabated unless federal laws are enacted to punish drunk drivers more severely, and truck drivers are forced to get enough rest in conformance with existing laws.

DRIVING ON EXPRESSWAYS AND LIMITED ACCESS HIGHWAYS

Limited Access Highways are those highways which do not allow the driver to exit, enter, or turn at will. Examples of these are Turnpikes and Interstates.

There are probably more people afraid to drive on limited access highways than the total sum of all of Michael Jordan's slam dunk shots and all other slam dunks made in the NBA. News of serious accidents discourages many from attempting to drive on these highways. In many instances getting to your destination is either impossible or difficult unless you use a limited access highway. If you are a busy person, using an expressway could save you valuable time.

If you can steer a vehicle precisely and have mastered driving at speeds of fifty to sixty miles per hour, you should be ready to tackle an expressway or interstate highway.

However, if you are a new driver and more than sixty years of age, it is arguable whether you should attempt it. If you are healthy, confident and have good vision, perhaps you can try. Ask your family or friends for their opinion. If you are not sure, call a reliable driving school and tell them to take you on an expressway.

A good plan for anyone who has never driven on an expressway is to first drive on a boulevard with a speed limit of forty-five to fifty miles per hour. When driving on a boulevard, the rules are the same as on the expressway. Stay in your lane and stay focused. Do not tailgate and leave plenty of space in front of you. Anyone who can drive on a boulevard at fifty miles per hour should be able to drove on any limited access highway. Be sure to practice changing lanes. Before you start on your great adventure, check the tires and clean the windows. If you are less than five feet three inches tall, you must sit on a cushion. You vision should be at least two inches above the steering wheel. Your seat belt must be used.

As you are entering the ramp, check the signs to be sure you are going in the proper entrance. Pause at the yield sign. Do not go because someone honks at you. Go only when you feel it is safe. If you have an acceleration lane you can usually enter without waiting since no vehicles will be coming behind you. However, after fifty to a hundred yards, you must merge quickly into the flow of traffic. The other drivers already on the highway usually allow you to blend into the stream of traffic.

If you do not have an acceleration lane you must be extremely careful before entering. You must look behind you and wait until no vehicle is coming for approximately one thousand feet (two city blocks). At this second, you must enter quickly and stay in the right lane. Once you have established your position, the rest is comparatively easy. Look well ahead in the center of your lane and maintain a speed of fifty or fifty five miles per hour. Stay five or six car lengths from the car in front of you. Glance in the rear and side mirror every five or ten seconds. Do not move the wheel when glancing in the mirror or when checking your speed. You should only glance in the mirror or check your speed for one second each time.

Passing a vehicle on the right is more hazardous because of the blind spot behind you. Never pass until you have thoroughly checked the front, rear and sides. Before you move out, be sure there is enough space between you and the vehicle you are passing. When you think you can pass, you must look in the rear mirror first. Now turn your head quickly over your right shoulder. Before passing look again. Be sure to look on the right beside you as well as behind you. If the traffic scene is clear, put on your right signal ten to twenty seconds in advance. Move out quickly. After you have passed the vehicle, move back into the right lane when you can see the car you have passed in your rear view mirror.

Do not be distracted by passing vehicles. Look in your lane. Do not change lanes unless it is necessary. Most exits will be on your right. This should pose no problem. A quarter of a mile before your exit slow down to forty miles per hour and put on your right signal. Usually a sign will show you the correct exit speed.

Sometimes an exit will be on your left. That means that two or three miles before your exit, you should be in the extreme left lane. Before changing lanes, signal well in advance. Glance in the rear mirror and side mirror. When no vehicle is in sight for at least 500 feet move over quickly into the left lane. When you are one quarter mile from the exit, put on your signal and slow down to forty miles an hour. As you enter the exit ramp obey the speed limit which should be twenty-five or thirty miles per hour.

It is recommended that for the first three or four times, you should not go at peak travel times. Consequently, your confidence will grow until you will no longer be afraid. It has been proven that in order to conquer a fear, you must try to do the very thing you are afraid of doing. Do not be an incomplete driver. Unless you are too panicky about it, follow the instructions and you will succeed.

HOW TO USE ANTILOCK BRAKES

Antilock brake systems are designed to prevent a vehicle's wheels from locking during emergency braking on slippery roads. Sensors near each wheel monitor rotational speed. As the brakes are applied and the wheel slows, an electronic control unit determines when any wheel is about to lock. The control unit then signals for reduced brake pressure, just enough to allow the wheel to start rotating again, thus preventing lockup.

An article in the Philadelphia Inquirer (December 1995) questioned the benefits of antilock brakes. In a study conducted by the Insurance Institute for Highway Safety, it was found that antilock brakes were not producing overall safety benefits. This study found that anyone inside a car with antilock brakes has a forty five percent greater chance of dying in a single vehicle crash by losing control and veering off the road.

The study also reported that the increased risk of death for anyone in a car with antilock brakes during a multiple-vehicle accident is six percent.

However, two auto industry associations released a study stating that vehicles with ABS had fewer accidents and injuries than those without them. This study showed an overall accident rate of nine to ten percent lower for cars with antilock brakes. Ironically, although this study conflicted with the insurance institute's study, no measurable difference was found in fatal car crashes.

These conflicting reports do not apply to large trucks and tractor trailers. Antilock brakes provide a clear safety advantage for these vehicles. Fleet managers report that antilock brakes have virtually eliminated crashes caused by jack knifed vehicles.

The insurance association declared that they do not know why antilock brakes are impressive on the test track, but not on the road. The answer could be that the drivers testing the antilock brakes know how to use them, but the majority of the driving public are not being instructed sufficiently.

It appears likely that many accidents with the ABS are occurring because the driver either pumps the brake or removes the foot from the brake pedal too soon. If you use the antilock brakes in an emergency situation, you must exert a firm continuous pressure on the brake pedal. The brake will pulsate rapidly, which means the ABS is working. At this time, it is imperative that you do not remove your foot from the brake pedal.

Hold it down and do not pump the brake.

With standard brakes experienced drivers were accustomed to pumping the brake gingerly on slippery roads since a heavy foot would cause the car to spin out of control. Pumping antilock brakes could result in eliminating all braking power. When the antilock brakes are activated, the system pumps the brakes faster than is humanly possible. Accordingly, the wheels unlock and the driver can retain steering control.

The effectiveness of anti-lock brakes has been enhanced by car commercials that imply that Antilock Brakes can prevent crashes because of better stopping power under all conditions. This is not completely true. On dry ground there is not much difference between standard brakes and Antilock Brakes. On slippery roads Antilock Brakes could make a difference. The Michigan State Police traffic crash unit found that ABS equipped vehicles could not make hard cornering maneuvers while braking as well as vehicles with standard brakes.

Many drivers do not know how to use antilock brakes and the manuals that come with their car offer little help.

Motorists feel secure with Antilock Brakes because of impressive advertising by the manufacturers. However, in a survey, it was found out that most drivers had little knowledge of how this technology works. Forty-five percent of the owners of vehicles with Antilock Brakes thought the brakes should be pumped on slippery roads. It is apparent that misinformed drivers think they are safer because they have antilock brakes. Therefore, they may become careless or not allow enough space in front of them.

At the present time it is obvious that antilock brakes are not the panacea that the manufacturers claimed them to be. Antilock brakes in certain situations with an uninformed driver, may actually contribute to an accident.

Although studies are continuing, it is evident that some changes in the ABS should be made and that drivers become more familiar with the proper use of the antilock system.

PEDESTRIANS VS DRIVERS

The only time most drivers yield to pedestrians when both have a green light is when an intersection is being policed by an officer or school guard. Additionally, many states have Cross Walks in highly traveled pedestrian walkways. These Cross Walks often appear in areas where there are no traffic signals. It is especially important for drivers to watch for pedestrians in these areas. If a pedestrian steps off the curb to cross the street, the driver must yield. Also, in business sections of large cities drivers will yield only when groups of people are already crossing the intersection. Otherwise, when an individual is crossing the street, the driver will seldom yield.

If pedestrians assume that drivers will not allow them to cross, they will almost always be correct. Drivers making turns at intersections pose a particularly dangerous threat to pedestrians, especially at night when vision is reduced. As a driver, you must always check for pedestrians before making your turn. If there are any pedestrians, you must yield. Remember, the pedestrians also have a green light and have the right of way according to the law.

Many drivers believe that pedestrians will yield rather than walk directly into the path of a moving car. The law is seldom enforced, and as a result, pedestrians are at the mercy of motorists. Many pedestrians are seriously injured or killed at night, especially on country roads. This is primarily due to the fact that these roads are poorly lit. When walking on country roads, it is important to walk against traffic and to stay as far as possible from the road.

Hopefully, readers of this book will obey the law and respect the rights of pedestrians.

CHAPTER 14
DRIVING A STICK SHIFT

Learning to drive a car with a manual transmission (stick shift) is not easy. For elderly people who never drove before, it is almost impossible. I strongly advise anyone over sixty to refrain from trying to learn to drive a stick shift car. With a stick shift car, you must use the clutch, the gas pedal, brake, shift gears, and steer simultaneously.

However, if you have never driven before, learn to drive an automatic transmission car first. This will give you more confidence to tackle the stick shift since you will know how to turn the wheel, steer, use the brake, etc.

Using your eyes correctly is just as important with the stick shift as it is with the automatic transmission car. Before moving the car, you should practice shifting gears without the motor running. While you practice shifting gears, also use the clutch. When you eventually start driving, you should not have to watch your hands while you are shifting gears. Therefore, become familiar with the different positions before starting to drive.

A long time ago the stick shift lever on American cars was on the floor. About thirty years ago, the lever was situated on the steering wheel. This type of stick shift uses a three-speed shift pattern because it has three forward positions, first, second, and third. There are not too many cars of this type in use today. Now American cars are made with four of five speed positions. The four-speed shift is the most desirable for older people. The five-speed is more complicated and young people who like sports cars would be more likely to purchase five-speed cars. Foreign sports cars have five speeds.

The "Reverse" position is not always in the same position in cars with manual transmissions. The pattern of the gears is usually disclosed on top of the knob of the gear shift lever.

FIG. 13 STICK SHIFT PATTERNS

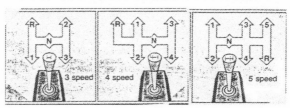

Study the stick shift pattern of the car you are going to drive. It is very unlikely that your car will have the three speed pattern used many years ago. If you know how to operate any one of the examples shown, you should be able to operate any stick shift car. Most American cars made recently use five speeds as shown. Therefore, the explanations given here will concern this particular stick shift pattern. Before beginning it is advantageous to know the following:

1.   All the general rules and guide lines that previously were defined for automatic transmission cars apply to stick shift cars.

2.   Before starting the engine the lever should always be in "N" or Neutral. Depress the clutch before starting the engine.

3.   Stick shift cars do not have a "Park" position so the parking brake must always be on before starting the car and applied after shutting off the engine.

4.   Before you come to a stop in first or second gear, the clutch must be depressed before the brake is applied.

5.   When driving faster in a higher gear, apply the brake first until you are going below fifteen miles per hour, then you apply the clutch before the car stops.

6.   The clutch does not stop the car. It prevents the engine from stalling when you stop.

7.   While driving in high gear, do not push the clutch in or keep your foot on top of it.

8.   When stopping the car in "Reverse", depress the clutch before the brake. Press the clutch slightly to keep the car under control as you go back in "R".

9.   Every time you stop, you must put the gear shift lever back into "Neutral" and begin again in first gear.

10.   If you turn the key in any gear but "N" the car will jump and stall unless your foot is on the clutch.

11.   If your clutch is depressed when you turn the key, the car will not jump no matter what gear you are in.

12.   Never shift gears unless the clutch is pushed in first.

13.   If you hear a grinding when shifting gears, stop shifting immediately. Be sure the clutch is depressed and shift gears again.

14.   You never push the clutch and gas pedal down at the same time.

15.   When shifting gears do not press the gas pedal down at the same time.

16.   When shifting gears do not press the gas pedal when pressing the clutch and do not depress the clutch when pressing the gas pedal.

17.   If your foot comes up too fast past the friction point (in first gear), the car will either stall or buck. If the car bucks, put your foot down on the clutch again and start again. The car does not stall or buck as easily in second gear. When you let the clutch up in third or fourth gear, the car should not stall. You also do not have to let the clutch

out as slowly in second gear and less slower in third and fourth gear.

18.   You do not use the clutch every time you use the brake. When driving in high gear and you want to slow down slightly, press the brake, slow down and go back to the gas pedal.

19.   If you are slowing down enough so the car starts to labor, you shift to a lower gear (downshift).

20.   Think of "Neutral" as being a bridge. When you go from second to third, you have to cross the bridge. Therefore, you should pause for a half a second before crossing the bridge. If you move the lever too fast, you will pass the bridge and the gears will not mesh causing a grinding sound.

21.   At certain times you will use the clutch alone, but you should never use the gear shift lever without engaging the clutch.

22.   First gear is used to get the car moving to a speed of ten miles per hour. Second gear is used to move the car to fifteen miles per hour. Third gear is for speeds up to twenty-five miles per hour. Fourth gear is for speeds more than thirty-five miles per hour and for highway driving. If the vehicle has five speeds, you use fifth gear for highway driving.

23.   If you have to stop in an extreme emergency do not be concerned about the car stalling. Use the brake alone as quickly as you can and do not worry about the clutch.

THE IMPORTANCE OF THE "FRICTION POINT"

It is extremely important to get the feel of the "friction point", especially when you let the clutch up in first gear. Once you get the car moving, it will not stall as easily when you shift into the other gears.

You are ready to start. Be sure your gear shift lever is in "neutral". Start the engine with your left foot pressing the clutch to the floor and right foot touching the gas pedal. Release the parking brake. Move the gear shift lever straight up to first gear with your right foot on the brake and your left foot on the clutch. The lever should go into first smoothly. If it does not mesh bring it back to "neutral" and try again.

Start raising your clutch (two inches) and at the same time, place your right foot on the gas pedal and press slightly. As you clutch comes to the "friction point", the car should start to move slowly. At this point, do not pull your left foot away from the clutch suddenly. As soon as you are moving five to ten miles an hour, you should be ready to shift into second gear. However, you are not going to do this now. In the beginning you are going to practice in first gear only so you can get the feel of the "friction point."

When the car starts moving, do not take your foot completely away from the clutch. It is not necessary to take your foot away before shifting into second gear because you stay in first gear only a few seconds. By not taking your foot off the clutch completely, the car will not stall as easily. When the car starts moving, keep your foot on the clutch at that point. If the car stalls while letting out the clutch, push the clutch back in, put your lever back in "neutral" and start all over. If the car starts to buck when you let out the clutch but does not stall, push the clutch in and let it out again as you press the gas slightly.

Once the car is moving in first gear about thirty feet, push the clutch in then apply the brake and stop. Put the lever back into "N" and start over. Continue to practice starting in first gear and stopping until you can do it without stalling.

Many new drivers stall in first gear because they are afraid to press the gas pedal. If the clutch comes up past the "friction point" without gas the car will stall.

Shifting Into Second Gear

Shifting the gear shift lever into first gear and then into second gear is relatively easy because you do not have to cross the neutral bridge to get to second gear. If you have mastered starting out in first gear, you are ready to try second gear.

When you are moving between five and ten miles per hour, push the clutch all the way in. At the same time do not feed any gas. Do not take your foot completely away from the clutch. This will prevent stalling or bucking. Now move the gear shift lever straight down to second gear with your clutch all the way down to the floor. Raise your clutch a little faster than you raised it in first gear and start feeding gas until you are moving to fifteen miles per hour. Practice starting out in first gear and going into second gear until you become proficient at it.

Shifting Into Third Gear

Shifting from second to third gear is more difficult because you have to cross the "neutral" bridge to get to third gear. In a four-speed car you will be driving in third gear most of the time except when you are driving on a highway, expressway or turnpike.

Now you are ready for third gear. Start out in first gear and go into second gear as explained. In second gear bring the speed to at least fifteen to twenty miles per hour. Push the clutch down to the floor and at the same time, stop pushing the gas pedal. To shift into third gear smoothly, do not push the lever too hard. As you come to the "neutral" bridge, pause for a half a second and move the lever to the right, then up to third gear. If the gears are meshing smoothly, you will not hear any grinding noise at all. Now raise your clutch all the way and feed enough gas so you will be driving about twenty-five miles per hour. Do not raise your clutch too slowly, but do not raise it too fast. Your foot should now be completely off the clutch. Continue to drive in third gear until you have to stop. Once you stop, you have to put your lever in "Neutral" and start from the beginning. The more you drive, the better you will become. After you drive for a while, you will shift gears automatically and will not have to think about every step you take. When driving on an open highway, do it in fourth gear. In a five-speed car (which is not recommended for older drivers). You drive mostly in fourth gear and use fifth gear for highways.

Downshifting

Every person who drives a stick shift car must be able to shift to a lower gear. Suppose you are driving at twenty-five miles per hour and you have to make a right or left turn. Your light is green so you do not have to stop. When you slow down to ten miles, you must shift to a lower gear or your car will start to labor and may possibly stall. Some cars can move without laboring at twelve miles per hour, others may start laboring in third gear at ten miles per hour. Your car will tell you this. If you feel the car start to labor at ten miles per hour, push your clutch in and move the lever carefully from third to second. Pause at the "neutral" bridge before pushing the lever into second gear. Do this before turning the corner. After you straighten out, step on the gas pedal again and when you reach twenty miles an hour, shift into third gear. Every time you have to slow down, you downshift to second gear or to first gear if necessary.

Reverse

The car should never be moving when you move the gear shift lever into "Reverse" . To go into "R" you have to use "Neutral" to get there. In some cars, you have to press down to get the lever to go into "R". Do not take your foot completely off the clutch when in "R". If you do, the car will have a tendency to move sporadically. You only spend a few seconds in "R" so you will not wear the clutch out if you keep your foot slightly on the clutch while the car is moving backwards. You can also pump the clutch slightly to control the speed of the car.

STARTING ON A HILL

This could be the most frustrating operation for the new driver to learn. There are two methods for starting on an upgrade. You do it with the parking brake or without it.

Without the Parking Brake

1. Shift into first gear keeping the clutch depressed and right foot on the brake.

2. Raise clutch almost to the friction point and hold it there.

3. Quickly take right foot away from the brake and step on the gas pedal (not too much).

4. As soon as the right foot steps on the gas pedal, raise the clutch pedal quickly just slightly above the "friction point" and hold it there.

5. As the car starts to go forward, press the gas pedal slightly and when the car is on ground level, shift into second gear.

Parking Brake Method

Some people prefer to start on an upgrade using the parking brake method. Put on your parking brake. Either you have the foot pedal type or the handle type which usually sits next to you on your right between the two front seats.

1. Shift into first gear, keeping the clutch depressed.

2. Raise the clutch almost to the friction point.

3.   Grasp the brake release of the car and slowly start to release it. At the same time, feed a little gas. As the parking brake is fully released raise the clutch enough to allow the car to move forward.

4.   Continue driving and shift into second gear.

It is not easy for a new driver to start up a hill with a manual transmission. When the car starts to roll back, the learner may step on the gas pedal too much without raising the clutch enough. The car will either stall or continue to roll back until the clutch is raised slightly above the "friction point". The new driver must step on the gas pedal quickly, but not too hard. Almost immediately after using the gas pedal, the learner must raise the clutch quickly, but not all the way. When you can raise the clutch to a certain point and keep a steady pressure on the gas pedal, the car can be made to neither go back or go forward. It will be perfectly balanced. Constant practice will enable you to master this difficult operation.

It is better to practice in the beginning with someone sitting beside you who knows how to drive a stick shift car. The part that frightens most learners is when the car rolls back too much. This could happen when the learner does not push the gas pedal or when the clutch is not raised enough. If the car stalls, use the parking brake and start all over. It is better to start on a slight upgrade at the beginning and when that is accomplished, go on to a steeper grade. In order to drive a gear shift car you must know how to start on an upgrade.

Driving a Gear Shift on Ice

Many drivers think it is best to drive on ice in first gear. This is a fallacy. The best way to drive on ice is to start out in second gear. This will decrease the tendency of the wheels to spin and better traction will be obtained. This procedure is also best on all slippery or wet roads.

CHAPTER 15

MOST FREQUENT MISTAKES MADE BY NEW
DRIVERS

Most people who have been driving for many years do not forget basic safety procedures. The obvious reason is repetition. They have been driving so long that they do not forget simple driving patterns. Repetition is the best antidote for forgetfulness.

However, the older neophytes tend to be forgetful for awhile until the various procedures become ingrained in their minds.

1. <u>ALWAYS START ENGINE IN "PARK"</u>

When starting the motor there is a tendency to move the lever to "D" instead of first turning the key while the indicator is in "P". Remember the motor can only be started in "P" or "N". Trying to start the engine in "D" or "R" is tantamount to trying to turn on a television set that is not plugged in. Nothing will happen. This is a safety feature. If the engine dies out and the lights turn red on the dashboard, you must start the motor by placing the indicator lever in "P" or "N". Do not place the lever in "P" if the vehicle is moving. It may damage the transmission. Push the brake to stop any movement of the vehicle and place the lever on "P".

When you are more experienced and the vehicle stalls while still moving, you can move the indicator to "N". Now you can turn the key and start the car without damaging the transmission while the car is moving. After the engine starts you can move the lever to "D" and continue driving.

2.KEEP FOOT FIRMLY ON BRAKE

After starting the engine in "P" position, be sure to place your right foot firmly on the brake pedal before moving the indicator lever to "D" or "R".

3.VEHICLE ROLLS WITHOUT PUSHING GAS PEDAL

When moving in a slow line of traffic (bumper to bumper) it usually is not necessary to touch the accelerator (gas) pedal. In most instances the vehicle will roll by itself. As the car rolls, keep your right foot above the brake pedal.

4.ALWAYS LOOK BEHIND YOU

When parked on the street never move out without looking behind you. If a vehicle is coming, do not go if the vehicle is moving fast. The speed of the approaching vehicle could be more important than its distance from you. It is better to wait until it passes you. Do not take chances.

5.DO NOT STARE AT STOP SIGNS

Staring at a distraction is a common mistake. When approaching a stop sign at an intersection, a new driver inadvertently stares too long at the stop sign. Consequently, the vehicle will drift too far to the right. While stopping for a stop sign or a traffic light, keep your vision straight ahead and when you glance left and right, do not move the steering wheel.

Many new drivers go too far to the right even when they do not stare at the stop signs. They instinctively try to move away from oncoming traffic.

6.PASS PARKED CARS BEFORE TURNING

If you are planning to execute a right turn at an intersection, do not lean to the right until you pass the last parked car on the right. After you pass the last parked car, you may turn your wheel slightly to the right. However, never get closer than three feet from the curb while turning.

If you drive too close to the curb, you are eliminating the necessary space cushion. You may drive up on the curb and possibly damage the vehicle.

7.DRIVING TOO CLOSE TO THE RIGHT

I have also observed many of my students going too far to the right even when there are no oncoming vehicles. I have found it necessary to move the steering wheel to the left many times to avoid striking a parked car. In this instance, the inexperienced older driver is completely oblivious of the danger involved.

This happens on a two-way street with parked cars on both sides of the street. There is enough space for your vehicle and one coming towards you. The street is approximately thirty feet wide.

When I remind my anxious students to drive close to the center of the street, they do it. However, if I say nothing, they veer to the right. Remember, you are sitting on the left side of the car. Therefore, your perception of the right side will be flawed. Focus your attention on staying close to the center of the street. At the same time, a vehicle coming towards you has the other half of the street. Do not stare at the oncoming vehicles. Do not look down in front of your car. Look straight ahead about half a block away occasionally glancing towards the center to see if you are staying close to the center.

I have repeated this many times in this book as well as pointing it out to my students. This fault seems to be very common among older new drivers. The solution is really not complicated. However, it requires total concentration at all times.

8.AFTER REVERSE, CHANGE LEVER

Whenever you move back in "Reverse", you must always remember to change the lever back to "Drive". When new drivers become distracted, they forget to change the lever. If this happens to an experienced driver, he will move the lever back to drive without thinking, because he senses the backward movement of the vehicle. However, the inexperienced driver may press the accelerator down and not recover in time to prevent an accident. In a moment of panic he or she may reach for the indicator lever instead of putting the foot firmly on the brake.

I have observed this situation many times while teaching novices. Remember, if you forget to change the lever back to "Drive", be sure to put your right foot firmly on the brake first.

BRAKING IS NOT ALWAYS THE ANSWER

Some new drivers have a tendency to brake too hard. To prevent a possible rear end collision, practice braking in a deserted area until you can stop gently. Suppose you are driving at twenty miles per hour through an intersection. Your traffic signal is green. As you are crossing, you notice a vehicle coming towards you from your right side. This driver has a red signal, but he is coming right at you. If you step on the brake, he will hit you right in the center of your vehicle. If you step on the gas pedal quickly, you may get out of the intersection without getting hit. This could happen to you because it happened to me. The man driving the other vehicle was on drugs and was apprehended after he struck another vehicle.

Most of the time, it is only necessary to touch the brake, but a nervous beginner could slam the brake and cause an accident. If you are approaching an intersection and someone unexpectedly turns left in front of you, touch your brake, but do not jam it. Usually you do not have to stop. Slow down. Remember there are cars behind you. New drivers must think of the rear as well as the front. If you stop suddenly, you could cause a chain collision.

If you are driving and a parked car starts to move out, do not immediately pounce on the brake. Touch the brake pedal and tap the horn.

If you are driving on a through street (no stop signs) and another vehicle seems to be approaching quickly from the side, do not jump hard on the brake. Ninety-nine times out of a hundred, the vehicle will stop especially if your street is well traveled. If you are concerned about this vehicle, tap the horn and place your foot over the brake pedal. When you are on a through street, the other side will always have a stop sign.

A TYPICAL ANSWER TO A COMMON MISTAKE

Although I have advised my students repeatedly to look in the center of their driving path and not to stare at distractions, some of my students have always found exceptions to this important rule. The scenario goes like this:

A boy is riding on a bicycle to the right of the student driver. She loses her composure, forgets my instructions and stares at the boy anxiously. The inevitable happens. She gravitates towards him.

Now I ask her this question, although I know her answer.

Question:"Why did you stare at the boy?"

Answer:"I did not want to hit him."

Another scenario goes like this:

I am parked on a narrow street with one of my favorite gray haired ladies. The street is one-way. Cars are parked on both sides of the street. There is space for one car to drive in the middle of the street. There is enough space to pull out of our spot as the car parked in front of us is six feet away.

She pulls out of the space, but instead of going towards the center of the street, she is going towards the parked car across the street. I tell her to stop and I say,

Question:"Why are you staring at the car?"

Answer:"Because I do not want to hit it."

Perhaps the most common mistake made by neophytes (and also some experienced drivers) goes like this:

I am instructing someone's grandmother how to control a vehicle. Everything is going along great until our vehicle starts veering to the right for no apparent reason. Of course, I know what my fearless companion is doing wrong, but I want to emphasize her mistake so I say,

Question:"Where were you looking just before we drifted to the right?"

Answer:"I was looking at the traffic light."

The answers all of these women told me has been repeated to me hundreds of times. The solution to the first two situations is the same. <u>You do not stare at the object you are trying to avoid</u>. You glance quickly at the object and then look where you want to go. Remember that you tend to go where you are looking. The woman who wanted to avoid the boy should have looked towards the left and steered gently towards the left side of her lane. A boy on a bicycle is only using about one foot of space.

The woman pulling out of the parking space must ignore the car parked on the other side of the street and aim for the center of the street.

I have demonstrated this by drawing an arrow on the street, showing the path the car should take. When the learner looks at the arrow her car always moves towards the center of the street between the parked cars.

If you are parked on the left side of a small street with parked cars, you may watch the left side of your car to see if you can clear the vehicle parked in front of you. After you clear the vehicle be sure to look in the middle of the lane. On a small street, do not look far away whether you are pulling out from the right or left.

The grandmother who stared at the traffic signal too long has to learn to glance at the light and immediately look in the center of her lane. Remember to glance quickly at the traffic signal and the stop sign. You can glance back at the traffic signal for a second, but only once at the stop sign since the stop sign is immobile.

DO NOT FAVOR RIGHT SIDE

Ask any neophyte driver which side they would favor when driving through a tight space and the answer would almost always be the right side. Inexperienced drivers automatically bear to the right in this situation. Perhaps it is because most people are right handed, or it may be a reflex action.

I would like to put that supposition to rest. When driving through a narrow space, you should always watch the left side of the vehicle. Therefore you are able to judge the left side better than the right side. It is extremely difficult for a novice to judge the distance on the right side.

If you are trying to go through a space that is eight or ten inches more than the width of your car, you should look out towards the left side. Stay four or five inches away from the object on your left and you will clear the space. Do not keep staring towards the left. Look towards the middle of the space to stay straight after you see that you are inches away from the left side. Move slowly. You must ignore the right side. Trying to judge the space on the right would be futile. Looking in the center of the space and glancing towards the left side will take care of this situation. Practically all new drivers fear driving through tight spaces. If you follow these instructions, you should be able to go through tight spaces successfully.

CHAPTER 16
TIPS FOR THE ELDERLY AND OTHERS

SCHOOL BUS

When a school bus stops with flashing red lights on top of the bus, you must stop at least ten feet from the bus. It does not matter from what direction you are coming, you must stop. If your traffic light is green you must stop. If you are coming from the side intersection, or if you are coming towards the bus, you must stop. When all of the children reach the pavement and the bus proceeds to move, you may also move, provided the top red lights are not flashing. You may go when you are on the other side of a divided highway. A divided highway is a two-way street divided by an island or a median strip. However, do not go even under this condition if the children are still crossing the street. Children do not know these rules. They may continue to walk through the median strip if it is not a physical barrier. Do not move until they cross the street.

FIG. 14 - STOPPING FOR SCHOOL BUS

EMERGENCY VEHICLES

When you hear a siren or see a vehicle with flashing lights behind you, pull over to the right if possible and stop. There will be times when you will not be able to pull over to the right. You will have to do what is best under the circumstances. Sometimes you have to move to the left to allow the emergency vehicle to get through. Other times you may not move at all. In situations like this, it is always better if you stay in the right lane. The right lane is the safest place to be for all slower drivers.

DO NOT OVERREACT

A new middle-aged driver may have a tendency to overreact under certain situations. Be very careful not to jam the brake unless you must avoid hitting something or someone. If you pay attention to your driving, you should never have to jam the brake unless an animal or person darts in front of you. When you are about to cross an intersection, do not panic when it appears that another car is not stopping on your left or right. If you are observant, you will know if the intersection is controlled by a four-way or a two-way stop sign. For an inexperienced driver it appears that the other driver is not stopping. Always be aware of the danger involved when you slam on the brake. You could cause a rear end collision.

The safe procedure is to place your right foot above the brake and glance quickly towards the car. If the car continues to move, tap the horn and slow down enough or stop if necessary. The driver behind you should see what is happening and should slow down. The bottom line is—think before you jam the brake pedal.

DO NOT LOOK INSIDE OF VEHICLE

Driving an automobile requires total concentration. Yet many people do not adhere to this basic rule. While driving, they allow something in their car to distract them and the inevitable happens. This unnecessary type of accident happens to experienced drivers. Many people tend to get careless behind the wheel. A driver could be distracted by a child. A bee flying into a vehicle could cause havoc. Therefore, it is tremendously important for the operator of a moving vehicle not to get distracted. If necessary, move over to the curb and stop, but do not panic. Losing control of the car could cause serious injury to people and property.

HOLD WHEEL STEADY WHEN DISTRACTED

Recently, the famous author, Steven King, was seriously injured while walking near his home. The man who was driving turned to see what his dog was doing in the back of the van. At the same time, he turned the wheel and struck Stephen King.

Recently in Philadelphia, a woman struck and killed a young man who was standing beside his disabled car. She made the mistake of turning her wheel sharply when she turned to look at her child in the rear of her car. The incident attracted much notoriety as she was the wife of an executive in a prominent Philadelphia organization. The moral of these true, unfortunate incidents is NEVER TURN THE WHEEL WHEN LOOKING BEHIND YOU, AND ONLY LOOK FOR ONE SECOND. When possible, pull over to the curb to take care of the problem.

PASSING A PUBLIC BUS

When passing a public bus, which has stopped near the curb to discharge passengers, pass carefully even though your traffic signal is green. Sometimes pedestrians dash in front of buses without thinking. When people get off a bus, they sometimes ignore traffic signals.

Just before you pass the bus, put your foot over the brake. Try to stay a few feet from the left side of the bus, so you have a little space to see better. Glance under the front of the bus so you might see someone's legs moving out into the street. You might also tap your horn. Drivers and pedestrians make mistakes. Be ready for this type of pedestrian error. It could save someone's life.

Do not pass a trolley car on the right which has stopped to take on or discharge passengers, even though the traffic signal is green. Wait until the trolley starts to move.

WATCH FOR PEDESTRIANS

It is extremely important to scan the entire traffic scene when waiting for a red light to change. Pedestrians, especially senior citizens sometimes start walking across the street after their signal light has changed to red. Some drivers have their eyes glued straight ahead and neglect to look left and right for pedestrians. A truck or bus could very easily be hiding a pedestrian, especially on your left.

LOOK TWICE BEFORE CROSSING INTERSECTIONS

When you stop for a two-way stop sign, you should be able to see at least one block in each direction. A good policy is to always look twice in both directions before

crossing. Once the road is clear, do not poke along. Cross
over about fifteen miles per hour.

<u>WHAT TO DO IF STOP SIGN OR TRAFFIC SIGNAL IS HIDDEN</u>

In cities every block intersection usually has some
means of traffic control. Either it is a four-way stop sign,
or a two-way stop sign or a traffic signal. If a bus or truck
is blocking your vision on the right, you immediately look
at the traffic signal on the left. If both sides are not visible,
touch your brake and try to see if the opposite traffic light
is working. If it is red, you know your light is green and
vice versa. If all the lights are broken, stop and go when it
is safe.

PICTURE 15 - HIDDEN STOP SIGN

Suppose you are approaching an intersection controlled by a stop sign. The stop sign on your right side is hidden. If you look diagonally from your right side to the other side, you see the back of a stop sign. Now you know that you have a stop sign on your right side.

TURNED AROUND STOP SIGNS

Did you ever get confused by stop signs facing the other way? When you come to an intersection and the stop sign is on your side but is not facing you, it is still your stop sign. Somehow it has gotten loose and the wind has turned it around. Sometimes you may see a stop sign on the other side of the intersection but it is facing you. This is not your stop sign. Your stop sign has to be on your side of the intersection. On some occasions it could be on your left on your side of the intersection because the right side may be hidden. The location of the stop sign tells you if it is for you.

160

PICTURE 16 - TURNED AROUND STOP SIGN

SPEED ZONE AHEAD

This means that you are entering an area with a regulated speed usually lower than the maximum speed of the state. It does not mean you will be permitted to drive fast.

POSITION OF "TURN ON RED" SIGNS

Unlike stop signs, rectangular signs are almost always posted securely to face the correct way. However, some inexperienced drivers are occasionally confused with signs which read "No Turn On Red". "No Turn on Red" signs must be facing you, either on your side of the intersection or across the street. The sign is usually placed near the traffic signal.

DO NOT JUMP WHEN DRIVERS BLOW HORN

Other drivers are too quick to honk at the slower driver. Many inexperienced drivers tend to get rattled when this happens. If this happens to you, do not automatically pull to the right. You may not have enough space to veer to the right. Stay calm and move over to the right only if you have space. Do not panic. There are certain drivers who try to pass everyone in front of them. Do not allow other drivers to force you to drive too fast. You must have control of your car. If you swerve into a parked car, it is your responsibility.

In my teaching experience, I have come across some people who constantly worry about the traffic behind them. Consequently, they drive too fast and they also turn corners too fast. Try to remember that the car must be under your control. When you turn at intersections you cannot go more than ten miles per hour. Think of it this way. Before you turn, you put on your signal. You slow down. Your brake lights go on. The driver behind you sees this. He will also slow down. If you are making a left turn, he will pass on your right. If you are making a right turn, he will pass on your left if he is in a hurry. Most of these drivers do not care about you. You must protect yourself. Drive with patience and think of yourself when you drive. Do not try to accommodate other drivers if it jeopardizes your safety.

TURN OFF MOTOR UNDER THESE CONDITIONS

People who drive usually supply transportation to their friends who do not drive. When letting your friends out of your car or into your car always turn off the motor and put the selector lever in "Park" position and keep your foot on the brake. Do not allow anyone getting out to move until you do this.

WHERE TO STOP FOR STOP SIGNS AND RED LIGHTS

When you stop at a stop sign, try to stop level with the sign unless there is a pedestrian walking. If you cannot see, roll out slowly until you can see in both directions. If both sides are clear, you should proceed. If not wait until you can cross safely. Be extra careful if parked cars are hiding your vision. You may have to roll out a little further so you can see.

When you stop for a red signal light, stop before the line of the pedestrian walk. You do not have to move out to the edge of the intersection because the traffic signal is controlling traffic. When the signal changes to green, start to move slowly looking left and right. Continue moving when you see the intersecting cars have stopped.

NEVER TURN LEFT IN FRONT OF MOTORCYCLES

Motor cycle riders cannot stop easily and they can lose their balance very easily. If you are making a left turn and a motor cycle is coming towards you within one hundred yards, do not turn in front of the motor cycle. Do not react towards a motor cycle as you would to an automobile. Motor cycles have their limitations.

FOUR WAY STOP SIGNS

At a four-way stop sign, every corner at the intersection has a stop sign. If two cars approach the intersection at the same time, the one on the right should go first. However, if cars approach the intersection a few seconds apart, the car which stopped first should go first. Drivers should go in the order in which they stopped. Some drivers do not observe this rule so if you stopped first, be sure the other driver is waiting as you proceed. Do not move if the other driver is aggressive and goes before you.

FIG. 17 - FOUR WAY STOP SIGN

HOW TO IDENTIFY A FOUR WAY STOP SIGN

As you approach an intersection which has a stop sign for you, glance to your left. If you see the back of a stop sign, at the intersecting street you know it is a four-way stop sign.

TWO WAY STOP SIGNS

There was a time long ago when four-way stop signs did not exist. Either there were traffic signals or two-way stop signs. Many residential areas are almost completely covered now with four-way stop signs. It is not uncommon to find an intersection with a two-way stop sign in the midst of an area replete with four-way stop signs. This could be dangerous. Many inexperienced drivers are lulled into believing that all of the streets in that particular area have four-way stop signs. Remember that all four-way stop signs are not marked. Therefore, if you are coming to an unmarked stop sign, look to your left and see if the street on your left has the back of a stop sign facing you. As you roll out after stopping, look left and right and then left again and proceed if you do not see anyone coming. Stop if you see a car while you are rolling out slightly since parked cars may obstruct your view. Do not assume that all corners with stop signs are four-way.

DO NOT SLOW DOWN WHEN BEING TAILGATED

If another driver is tailgating you, do not deliberately slow down. The other driver could be intoxicated or on drugs. This could be an explosive situation. Continue driving in your normal manner.

USE BRAKE TO SLOW DOWN

When moving more than twenty miles an hour, going downhill or turning around a corner too fast, you must use the brake to slow down. Many new or inexperienced drivers think that not using the gas pedal is enough to slow down. Not so. A body in motion at a certain speed will continue to move at that speed and in the same direction until an outside force is applied. This is called the law of "inertia" and the outside force used to slow down the vehicle is when you use the brake pedal. When going downhill, the force of gravity makes the car go faster. Therefore, you must use more pressure on your brake pedal and use it sooner.

LETTING CARS OUT OF DRIVEWAYS

You are driving on a busy street with shopping sections and lots of driveways. As you are driving you notice many drivers waiting at driveways for the opportunity to exit. Should you stop or should you continue? According to the rules, the driver of the car in the driveway should wait until the way is clear. Some good hearted drivers stop and let these cars go out in the street. If the traffic is bumper to bumper and the cars are moving a few feet at a time, you can allow a car to get in front of you. However, if the traffic is moving smoothly at twenty miles per hour or more, it could be hazardous to stop in the middle of the street. You could get hit in the rear. If you want to be a good Samaritan and let someone in, be sure the car in back of you is not near you and not moving fast. Do not stop unless you are positive it can be done safely.

LETTING PEDESTRIANS WALK IN FRONT OF YOU

Do not tell pedestrians to walk in front of you when they have a red light. If you want to allow a pedestrian to walk in front of your car, you must be one hundred percent positive that there are no other cars coming into your intersection. Sometimes a car will be turning into the very area that the pedestrian is walking. It is better for pedestrians to wait until it is legally safe to cross the street. If someone wants to cross in the middle of the street, it could be dangerous for you to stop especially if other cars are behind you. If you notice an elderly person walking in the middle of the street, not looking left or right be careful. Pump your brake a few times so the driver in back of you knows you are stopping and motion for other drivers behind you to slow down. It is also advisable to tap your

166

horn lightly a few times to alert the elderly person and the other drivers.

TURN IGNITION OFF WHEN GETTING GASOLINE

It is hazardous to let the motor run when gasoline is going into your gas tank. Always turn off the ignition and put the indicator lever in "P". No one should be smoking a cigarette outside while the gasoline is entering the gas tank.

HAVE CAR CHECKED PERIODICALLY

Most cars that are two or three years old should not use more than one quart of oil for every two thousand miles. Sometimes you might have a car that is burning too much oil. Have your car checked every month or every two hundred mile interval. Have the oil and oil filter changed every two thousand miles together with a lubrication. Have your radiator flushed and drained every two years and replace the anti-freeze. In the winter have your anti-freeze checked. Every few months ask your mechanic to examine your belts and hoses. Do not drive around with too little air in the tires. Before getting in your car look at the tires to see if any of them are low. You do not have to be a mechanic to drive a car. Try to find a reliable service station . If possible join an automobile club for emergencies.

GETTING OUT OF A TIGHT SPACE

You park your car on the street and when you come back, you find your car wedged in between two vehicles. Do not panic. There is a simple way to extricate your car, even though you only have a few inches of space to get out.

1.   In "R", let the car roll back with your foot above the brake. Do not be concerned if your car touches the vehicle behind you. When bumpers barely touch there is no damage. Try to go back straight. Do not turn the wheel towards the curb unless the rear tires of your car were pointing to the left.

2.   Keep your foot firmly on the brake pedal and move the indicator lever to "D". Assuming you are on the right side of the street, turn the wheel as far to the left as you can with your foot on the brake so the car does not move.

3.   Now allow the car to roll with your foot resting above the brake pedal. When you can see that you are close to the car in front of you, press the brake and stop.

4.   With your foot on the brake, put the lever in "R". Turn the wheel to the right as far as it goes with your foot on the brake so the car does not move.

5.   Now let the car roll back slowly with your foot above the brake pedal. When you have gone back as far as you can or if the right rear tire is touching the curb, press the brake and stop.

6.   Put the lever back in "D" and turn the wheel to the extreme left following the same procedure as explained before. If you still cannot get out repeat everything over again.

7.   When you finally get out, do not turn the wheel back too soon. Get well away from the parked car before you straighten out your car.   However, try not to go out into the other half of the street if it is a two-way street.

Whenever you park your car on the street, be sure you do not park too close to the curb. Try to be no closer than three or four inches from the curb. If your tires are extremely close to the curb and you are wedged in between two cars, you may not be able to get out. When you turn the wheel, the tires near the curb will strike the curb and you will be immobile until the car in front or behind you moves.

ANGLE PARKING

All large shopping center parking lots have angle parking. You must know how to park between the lines and to be able to back out safely when you leave.

FOLLOW THESE RULES WHEN PARKING ON THE RIGHT SIDE

1.   Go as far to the left as you can keeping the car straight.

2.   Moving slowly, turn the wheel when the front of your car starts to pass the first line of the lane you have chosen.

3.   As you turn, look into the center of your lane.

4.   Your foot should be resting above the brake pedal.

5.   Move slowly to the front of your parking space while looking in the center of the lane.

FOLLOW THESE RULES WHEN PARKING ON THE LEFT SIDE:

1.Go as far to the right as you can, keeping your car straight.

2.Moving slowly, turn the wheel when the front of your car starts to pass the first line of your parking lane.

3.As you turn look into the center of your lane.

4.Enter the lane slowly with your foot over the brake pedal.

5.Move slowly into the front of your parking space, and continue looking at the center of your lane.

When you leave your parking space be sure to back out straight if another vehicle is parked alongside of you. Do not press the accelerator if the car moves.

WEAR SEAT BELTS

Get in the habit of wearing your seat belt every time you drive. Be sure the lap belt is fairly tight but comfortable. The belt should not be across your abdomen, but should rest below your hips. The shoulder harness should not be too loose. Feel comfortable so your driving posture will not be restricted

When anyone is involved in an accident there are two crashes. The most important one is the second one which happens inside the car. After a car slams into an object like a tree, the passengers in the car continue to move forward until they slam into the wheel, dashboard or windshield. It is this second collision which causes serious injury or death. Another result of violent accidents occurs when the occupants of the car are thrown completely out onto the road. Many a person has walked away from a total wreck unharmed because he was wearing a seat belt. There are some accidents where the seat belt does not help, but overall your chances of survival are much greater with the seat belt.

TURNING INTO TRAFFIC

A "T" intersection is one in which your street ends and you must make a right or left turn. On this type of intersection you must yield to all intersecting traffic unless the intersection is controlled by a traffic signal.

If you are a new driver, you obviously cannot turn around corners quickly. It would probably take a senior citizen five to eight seconds to complete a right turn and not hinder a vehicle coming from the left at forty miles an hour. Therefore, a half a block of space would not be enough to execute a right turn safely. The vehicle on your left should be almost one block away before you turn.

Many novices think they can go if they see a half a block or less of space. They do not realize that the other vehicle is moving quickly and in a few seconds the space is gone. Their perception of the approaching auto's speed fools them. At forty miles an hour, a vehicle travels one block in approximately nine seconds. It is difficult for a new driver to estimate an approaching car's speed.

A left turn at a "T" intersection is more dangerous than a right turn since vehicles are coming from your right and your left. You need more time to execute the left turn. If another vehicle is approaching at forty miles an hour, you will have to move faster to turn safely. Never begin your turn if the vehicle is less than a block away. If you see a vehicle speeding, do not go. Wait until it passes you. When you have more experience, your judgement will be better and you will know when you can turn safely.

USE MIRRORS WHEN DRIVING

This is so important that it must be repeated. Every time you put your foot on the brake, look in the mirror. Every time you are about to make a left turn or a right turn, look in the mirror. While driving straight ahead, look in the mirror every ten seconds. Always know what is behind you. Take quick glances. Do not stare. New drivers have a tendency to only look in front of them. There are four places that affect your driving space. Front, rear, left side and right side. Therefore, do not make a movement of any kind unless you look in the rear mirror, your left side mirror if you are going to the left, and look over your right shoulder if moving to the right.

DO NOT GET MOVING VIOLATIONS

If you commit a moving violation you will be assessed points. Different states have their own rules. Usually, if you are charged with a certain number of points, you will be asked to take a re-examination. Although these tests are not difficult, elderly people dread the thought of these examinations. Moving violations are usually the following:

1.   Entering the wrong way into a one-way street.
2.   Making a left turn where it is not permitted.
3.   Going through a red traffic signal.
4.   Going through a stop sign.
5.   Exceeding the speed limit.
6.   Driving below the minimum speed.
7.   Reckless driving.
8.   Drunken driving
9.   Being involved in an accident in which you are completely at fault.

There may be other reasons, but these are the most prominent. You do not get points for parking violations.

MORE TIPS FOR NEW AND OLD DRIVERS

1.   Always carry an extra set of keys. Someday you will be glad you did.
2.   If you are confused about traffic signals, pretend you are walking. The rules are the same.
3.   Never pass another car at an intersection.
4.   Never pass on a curve or on a hill.
5.   Drive on the right in the first lane next to the parked cars.

6.   If your car breaks down, pull up your hood and put on your hazard lights. Try to park on the extreme right if possible.

7.   If you are tired or drowsy, stop and rest.

8.   If there are others in your car do not join in conversation with them.

9.   Never remove the cap from an overheated radiator. Do not continue to drive. Wait for the radiator to cool down. Go to the nearest service station.

10.   Do not drive after taking medicine which makes you drowsy.

11.   If you have impaired hearing, use your eyes more.

12.   If a driver behind you is impatient pull over to the right and let him pass.

13.   Stay away from heavy traffic until you feel confident. Go into more traffic gradually, as your driving improves.

14.   After a rain or snow storm clean the headlights.

15.   Do not smoke while driving.

16.   When you know you have to make a left turn, go in the lane near the middle of the street at least two blocks before the intersection. Stay on the right when you have to make a right turn.

17.   If you are not in the proper lane to make a turn and traffic is heavy, do not force your way into the lane. Drive ahead and turn in the next convenient intersection.

18.   Never shift into "Park" while the car is moving or the transmission will be severely damaged.

19.   When driving bumper to bumper in a slow moving line, do not push the gas pedal. Most cars will roll slowly without using the gas pedal.

20.   Do not drive with under inflated tires. Low tire pressure can cause tire failure. The car will handle better

with properly inflated tires. Tires should have at least twenty-eight pounds of air pressure.

21. Your foot does not always have to be pressing the brake or the accelerator. There are times when your foot will be pressing neither one.

22. When stopping behind a car, stay one half of a car length away. You should be able to see the rear tires of the car in front of you.

23. To start up on a very steep hill begin by putting your left foot firmly on the brake pedal. Step on the gas pedal slowly and then release your left foot from the brake pedal. The car should proceed up the hill without slipping back.

24. A green arrow pointing straight ahead means that you cannot go left or right, but only straight ahead.

25. A delayed green light means that the traffic signal for the cars coming towards you turns green before yours does.

26. Do not put high octane gasoline in a four cylinder vehicle. Use eighty-seven octane regularly.

ICY ROAD HAZARDS

Many pedestrians especially children and older people do not realize the extreme danger they face when they walk in front of motor vehicles on icy roads.

Recently in Philadelphia, a boy was killed and his twin brother was critically injured because they stepped in front of a bus. The bus driver lost control of the bus and skidded into the boys. Many people including those who drive automobiles foolishly step in front of moving vehicles traveling on icy roads.

HOW TO COPE WITH TRUCKS AND TRACTOR TRAILERS

Many automobile drivers are unaware that trucks and buses have three blind spots behind them. One blind spot is when you are in the left lane next to the truck or bus. The driver may not see you if you are too close to the left side of his vehicle.

Another blind spot occurs when an automobile stays too close on the right side of the truck or bus. A car in this position is probably less visible to the commercial driver than a car on the left side. The driver of the automobile should stay as close as possible to the right edge of the lane and move away as soon as possible.

The third blind spot is directly behind the truck or bus. Automobile drivers should not stay too close to the rear of the truck or bus since they are not visible to the commercial driver. These drivers also cannot observe the traffic scene ahead.

Tractor trailers and large trucks pose a greater hazard at night than during the day. The tail lights on most tractor trailers are smaller than those on many passenger cars. Therefore, passenger car drivers have to be especially careful on dimly lit roads. It is mandatory for trucks to have bars in the rear to prevent "under ride" collisions. However, many trucks and tractor trailers do not have side bars or side lights making it very hazardous for drivers when the trucks are backing out on a dark road.

When driving in a city or town, do not stay on the right side of a large truck. When a truck driver has to make a right turn, he swings to the left. He may not see you on his right side. Many a car driver has been jammed between a truck and the curb.

The best way to avoid a collision with a truck is to stay away from it as much as possible. When you are passing a truck or bus be sure to accelerate so you can move quickly away from the blind spot. Do not slow down. Remember that a tractor trailer going at a high speed may not be able to slow down enough if you reduce his braking distance. After passing never pull back in front until you can see the truck or bus in your rear view mirror. As soon as you can, move into another lane.

Any time you have to decelerate unexpectedly on a highway, look behind you. If a truck is behind you and you are unable to change lanes, put on the hazard lights, open the window and wave you arm up and down.

Since most highways do not provide separate lanes for trucks, accidents with other vehicles are inevitable. The present apathy towards truck related fatalities must be addressed. Unfortunately, Congress will not act unless enough pressure is applied by the public. A good beginning would be for truck drivers to abide by the speed limit and drive only in the right lane. Present laws should be enforced and stronger laws should be enacted for the safety of the public and the truck driver.

CHAPTER 17
MORE ADVENTURES OF FOUR WHO DARED TO DRIVE

Amy was a pretty eighteen year old young lady who wanted to drive. There was one catch. She had a learning disability. If you met Amy and spoke to her, you would never suspect there was anything wrong with her. She was not stupid, but she had difficulty learning something new. She had graduated from high school and was preparing to go to a college in Florida which specialized in teaching people with learning disabilities.

Amy needed something to bolster her confidence in herself and driving an automobile seemed to be the answer. Her parents were a hundred percent behind her.

I soon discovered that I had to proceed very slowly. In the beginning I concentrated only on steering. We did not try any right or left turns. She pleasantly surprised me by being able to stay in her lane after three hours of driving. Her motor skill was good. She was not awkward and was involved in sports.

When I tried to teach her hand over hand turning for right turns and left turns we had a problem. She could not seem to get the knack of turning hand over hand. At one time she broke down and cried out of frustration.

I took her into an empty school yard, determined not to leave until she mastered hand over hand turning. I told her to hold the wheel. I place my left hand over her left hand and my right hand over her right hand. Now I told her to make "U" turns. We turned the wheel with my hands on her hands. At the same time, I made sure we turned the wheel hand over hand. We repeated this procedure twenty or thirty times. I took my hands away from the wheel and told her to try it herself. She was not perfect, but after a while she started to do it correctly.

I discovered that she could learn a new operation by constant repetition. Now that she knew how to turn the wheel, I was ready to take her into a quiet area to practice left and right turns. It took her longer than usual, but eventually she mastered it.

Going back in reverse was a problem, but she persisted and eventually was able to do it fairly well. I started to take her into a little more traffic. At first she was afraid of left turns when cars were coming towards her. Almost all new drivers are afraid of this, but Amy was more fearful than the average driver. She was so motivated that she never thought of quitting. We kept doing left turns until most of her fear was eliminated.

Amy needed thirty-six hours of driver training before I felt she could drive. To take the driving test in Philadelphia you must drive through an obstacle course while staying in the proper lane at all times. Included in the test was a serpentine (zig zag) and a turn about in a stall measuring twenty-eight feet in width and thirty-five feet in length.

The test could be confusing for anyone and doubly so for Amy. We stood at the side of the course for one hour and watched people taking the test. I answered all her questions until she told me she understood the test course. She took the examination and was perfect. When I told the examining officer Amy had a learning disability, he could not believe it.

Amy is a real person. This is true as are all of the examples in this manuscript. People with handicaps are usually more motivated than those with no handicaps. Fear is not a physical handicap and can be overcome.

I do not know if Amy will ever be able to drive alone. Her driving will be limited, but having a driver's license will do wonders for her psyche.

Janice was seventeen years old when she learned how to drive. One day she was turning right into a narrow street and came very close to an approaching vehicle. The driver of the car swore at her so angrily that afterwards she was afraid to drive.

Janice got married and thought she had no need for driving. Her husband enjoyed driving and did not push her to learn. Twenty years went by, her husband started to complain about his back. It was discovered that he had a tumor in his spine. It was not malignant, but it was deemed inoperable. After a while, his condition worsened and he could not walk.

Janice started to take driving lessons. Her aptitude for driving was not great, but she had made up her mind. She had no choice–she had to learn. Janice was a very capable person and held a very good position with the city. She could only go out for a lesson once a week. Every Saturday, Janice went out with me. Her husband had to be taken for therapy three times a week. While learning she paid someone to take her husband for therapy. She did not learn quickly, but she persisted and is now taking her husband to different places. If her husband was a well man, she probably would still not be driving. It is better to learn before an emergency arises.

Nancy had a problem. She graduated from college but did not have any desire to work. She did not know what she wanted to do. In the meantime she was imbibing alcoholic beverages too freely. The inevitable happened. One night while driving alone, she slammed into a tree and was propelled out of the car. For a while her life hung in the balance. After many months of hospitalization and rehabilitation she was sent home.

Because of the accident, she could hardly see out of her right eye and Nancy's father became very concerned about her. She moped around the house and seemed despondent. She finally admitted to him that she wanted to drive, but was afraid to try.

After talking to her doctor, they both concurred that she had to overcome her fear as part of her rehabilitation. Her father and I convinced her to try. The first time she tried to drive she was almost shaking with fright. After a few minutes, she composed herself. We stayed in quiet areas and she gradually became more confident.

Since her vision on the right side was almost gone, I advised her to favor her left side. If we were on a street with marked lanes, I told her to look in the middle of the lane and never to watch the right side. When going through a narrow space, she was told to stay close to the object on her left. On a two-way street with space for parked cars and a car going in both directions, she stayed near the middle. It was fortunate for this young lady that the sight in her left eye was not impaired. The right side of the car is more of a blind spot for all drivers so she could manage with the sight in her left eye. Nancy is happy now and is going back to school with the intention of helping handicapped children.

Dorothy's husband did not like to drive. He only drove when he had to. He had been driving for a few years in Canada when he and Dorothy decided to move to an area near Philadelphia.

He was very anxious for Dorothy to drive. Like many people, Dorothy at age thirty-two was afraid to drive. However, he insisted. She took a few lessons from a driving school.

They were both fond of camping. One week-end they decided to go camping in Pennsylvania. After stopping at a rest station on Route 80, Dorothy's husband made a drastic mistake. He asked her to get behind the wheel.

Route 80 is no place for a beginner. The cars and trucks move fast. Most of them exceed the fifty-five mile speed limit. As soon as she entered the highway her husband realized his mistake. He prodded her to go faster, but the faster she went, the more nervous she became. Poor Dorothy was panic stricken. There was no way out. She had to drive to the next exit which was twelve miles away. Dorothy was in tears. Somehow she managed to reach the exit safely.

After this horrendous experience Dorothy wanted no part of driving. She found a good position in Philadelphia. There she met a young lady, a former student of mine, who convinced Dorothy to try again. I gave Dorothy a driving lesson and found her to be nervous, but her motor skill was good for a beginner. She seemed to be hesitant about continuing to take more lessons. I told her she would lose most of her fear if she would take driving lessons regularly. Evidently I was not persuasive enough. I did not hear from her again for two years.

In the meantime, her job duties changed. Now she had to visit parents to help them cope with babies born with serious handicaps. Some of these babies were born with cerebral palsy, epilepsy, or autism, etc.

My former student kept encouraging her and she finally called me. In the beginning she was very jumpy, but as the lessons progressed she started to gain confidence. Eventually she started her driving lessons from her workplace. She would then drive to her house which involved going through heavy traffic.

As time went by she became very enthusiastic about driving. She passed the driving test on her first attempt.

Now when she and her husband take trips, Dorothy does half of the driving which makes her husband happy.

Dorothy's experience proves that fear of driving or fear of almost anything can be overcome by determination, tenacity and desire.

CHAPTER 18
BE A HAPPY NEIGHBORHOOD DRIVER
AND ANOTHER INTERVIEW WITH A
RECOVERED PHOBIC DRIVER

This segment is devoted solely to the countless numbers of demoralized women left helpless by the death or debilitating illness of their spouses. They desperately want to drive, but their fear has overwhelmed their urgent need to drive. To many, the dread of driving on a busy expressway or turnpike is too traumatic. However, these highways with their breakneck pace and turmoil, are not essential modes of transportation for older people.

The message I want to convey to these women is that they can be neighborhood drivers and be happy. Their mental anguish can be ameliorated partially by comparing steering a shopping cart to driving an automobile. Although pushing a shopping cart is not life threatening it is somewhat analogous to driving an automobile.

A women pushing a cart in a supermarket can have a minor accident if she does any of the following:

1. Moves too fast
2. Doesn't look where she is going
3. Exits from an aisle without looking for other people.
4. Double parks her cart
5. Allows her children to distract her attention
6. Does not stay focused.

If you are careful and alert, driving in your neighborhood can be as accident free as pushing a cart. This means driving at a safe speed, stopping at stop signs, red lights and observing traffic regulations. People who are careful drivers usually do not have accidents in their own neighborhood. Driving in a familiar area will also boost their confidence.

Do not let your age discourage you. Many women who are driving today learned in their sixties and early seventies. The rewards of being independent are worth the angst you may suffer while trying to drive.

I know of women who after driving in their neighborhood experienced a dramatic increase in their confidence. Afterwards, many of them were able to explore areas further away.

Don't be overly concerned about driving away from your neighborhood unless you feel ready to take the plunge. Otherwise, stay in your neighborhood. The joy of being able to get behind the wheel and visit friends, shops, supermarkets, etc. is within your reach. Your impossible dream is possible. Do it now. Don't procrastinate any longer. There is no secret formula or magic wand that can transform you into becoming a proficient driver. Follow the directions in the chapter entitled "How to Get Started". Making excuses like "it's too hot", or it's too cold", or "I'll wait until the spring" is self defeating. Do not evade the issue.

The true experiences of the people depicted in this book should be an incentive and inspiration for every reluctant woman afraid to drive.

I believe that some women can be too serious-minded. They dwell too much on the dangerous consequences of driving an automobile. If you are in this category—lighten up! Conversely, women who are light hearted and laugh easily usually are not so fearful of driving.

Any woman who has a spouse who is permanently unable to function mentally or physically has an obligation not only to her partner, but to herself. Instead of wallowing in her misfortune, she should do the right thing.

You don't have to be an engineer to drive an automobile. Most people can learn to drive safely with the proper guidance. Make up your mind to do it now, not next week, or next month, but, NOW!

Recently I had the opportunity of interviewing a former student who was a classic example of a phobic driver. She had leased a new car and wanted to take me for a ride while I reviewed the car's manual with her. Afterwards, I interviewed her.

Question:Were you always afraid to drive?

Answer:Yes. I tried to drive as a teenager but my mother discouraged me. She always worried that I would have an accident.

Question:Did you continue to drive?

Answer:No. I stopped after two years. My mother's apprehension affected me.

Question:What happened after that?

Answer:I didn't try to drive again until I was married for thirty years. My husband was not in good health and I felt that someday, I would have to drive. He tried to help me, but he was too nervous. I decided to go to a driving school.

Question:How did you do?

Answer:Not too well. I always had a headache on the day of my lesson. My fear of having an accident was overpowering. I could not continue.

Question:Did you have any other fears about driving?

Answer:Yes. I was terrified when I had to drive up or down a steep hill and the thought of driving on a narrow bridge frightened me. I was also afraid of left turns in heavy traffic.

Question:When did you try to drive again?

Answer:I knew that I had to drive so I took another refresher course. However, I gave up again. I couldn't take the anguish that was brought on by driving or the thought of driving.

Question:What made you get started again?

Answer:My husband had a series of mini strokes and for a while was not able to drive. I was getting desperate. A friend of mine told me about Norman Klein, who had a reputation for helping nervous drivers. I contacted him and proceeded to take three lessons a week. I found him to be very understanding. I did better with him than before, but as time went by, I started to take fewer lessons even though my driving was improving. Norman told me that because of my husband's ill health if I didn't drive now, I would have to rely on other people to help me.

Question:What did you decide to do?

Answer:I knew he was right. I asked him to make a recording with his words of encouragement. Before I went driving, I listened to his message on the tape so it would inspire me.

Question:What happened to your husband?

Answer:His health deteriorated so that he could no longer drive. Now I knew I had to drive. I had no choice unless I paid someone to do my shopping and to take my husband to various doctors. I could not afford that. I drove with Norman to all the places I would have to go to including food stores, doctors and hospitals.

Question:Did you finally get rid of all your fears?

Answer:I still get a little nervous before I drive but once I get behind the wheel I feel more confident and am able to drive.

Question:Do you think you will ever be rid of your fear?

Answer:I'm not sure, but as of now I am managing very well. Occasionally, I ask Mr. Klein to accompany me to a destination I am not familiar with. He told me that as I drive, I will continue to improve until most of my fear will disappear. I don't lie awake at night anymore and I don't get headaches worrying about driving.

Question:Do you have any advice for people who are afraid to drive?

Answer:I felt that there was no way I would ever drive. I thought no one could be as frightened as I was. I was wrong. It took me three years under the tutelage of Mr. Klein to conquer my fear, but it was worth it. If I could do it, I believe anyone can. I don't think I would be driving today without Mr. Klein's patience and guidance. I am proof that if you don't give in to your fear, you too will be able to drive.

CHAPTER 19
CONCLUSION

Below is a summary of important rules to remember when driving:

1.   Look straight ahead into the middle of your lane.
2.   Always stay in your lane even if you think you are alone.
3.   Never, never go out of your lane unless you check the rear three times.
4.   Never stop suddenly unless it is to avoid hitting something.
5.   Glance in the rear mirror every ten seconds.
6.   Never stare in the mirror or at a distraction for more than one second.
7.   Do not let drivers behind you force you to cross yield signs or stop signs when it appears risky to do so. Let them honk!
8.   Before you drive, check your tires, mirrors, get comfortable and use your seat belt.
9.   Always be in control of your car. You do not have to keep up with other drivers.
10.   Do not neglect practicing "Reverse". Know which way to turn the wheel when going backwards.

If you are still hesitant about learning how to drive, look deep into your psyche. How much do you want to drive! Unless you have some type of handicap which physically or mentally precludes you from driving, are too old (over seventy-five) or a complete "Klutz", there is no valid reason for you not to drive.

In wars, pilots are jittery before every mission. The men who went to the moon were apprehensive about the perilous journey, but they were eager to go. You do not have to fly to the moon, and you do not have to go on a life threatening mission. Learning to drive is within your grasp. There are many people who were not natural born drivers, but they persevered and became capable drivers.

When Jack learned how to drive, his daughter, Elaine realized that she also had to try to learn. She felt that if her father with all his fears and phobias could learn, so could she.

Elaine was just as frightened and nervous as her father, but her youth was in her favor.

This young lady had the least amount of knowledge about traffic rules and regulations than anyone I had ever taught. She had seldom been a passenger in a vehicle. Her family did not use automobiles as a form of transportation. She was very unobservant the few times she had been a passenger in an automobile. Elaine was also very naive. She could not understand why some people did not observe the rules of driving.

I recognized from the beginning that she was not a "natural driver". In the beginning, Elaine did not realize that she had to use the brake to slow down when going down a hill. Other times she would turn around corners too fast making the car go out too wide. These mistakes are symptomatic of a neophyte driver who does not have good "motor skills."

In the beginning, Elaine had no feel for driving. Her steering was erratic and she had a tendency to stare at distractions instead of looking in her lane. She became discouraged. I advised her to continue since she did show improvement. If she waited, learning to drive would be more difficult. Elaine took my advice. She started to improve. One day she told me, she drove for thirty miles on a highway towards Atlantic City.

Elaine, like many others I taught proved that even if you are not a natural born driver, you can learn if you are highly motivated. She took many lessons, but now knows when to press the brake and learned how to steer the car. It cost her more than she wanted to spend, but what she accomplished will last her a lifetime.

Elaine had a friend who had been trying to learn to drive for a year without success. Coincidentally, Bea had the same problems that plagued Elaine. She could not stay in her lane. Her right turns were too wide so she wound up on the left side of the street. Her father could not cope with her poor driving. He did not know how to correct her driving so he mistakenly told her to watch the center of the car. When she did this her driving worsened. Bea also tried to keep the steering wheel in a straight position even when the street was on a curve or angle.

Bea and Elaine's driving shortcomings were typical of many people who had tried to drive, but were not successful. People who are not coordinated have to be coached properly. A novice who tries to make a right turn by pushing the gas pedal too hard before turning the wheel finds herself on the wrong side of the street. If she is not told about her mistake, she may not improve and will think she can never learn. Bea and Elaine would never have become capable drivers if they had not received proper instruction and encouragement.

Driving did not come easy for these two eighteen year old girls, but their desire to drive motivated them enough to learn. If you are afraid that you cannot learn, or if you once tried, try again. Perhaps you also pushed the gas pedal too much before turning corners. Perhaps you also watched the car instead of the road.

In a quiet area, make zig-zag marks on the ground by drawing 10 chalk lines that are a few feet long and about fifteen feet apart. If you can guide the car on the marks, you can learn to steer. Do not forget to look at the chalk lines and guide your body towards them. When you can put the car where you want to go, you can drive. Simply phrased, learning to drive is learning to steer. The rest is following traffic rules and regulations. It is very seldom that a person cannot learn to steer a vehicle.

Suppose you have no problem steering a car, but your fear of driving overpowers you. Do you remember how nervous you were when you began a new job? As time went by, you became more confident and eventually your anxiety disappeared. After six months of driving your fear will diminish. You will realize that driving an automobile is within your reach. You will be an independent person. To learn to drive, you must have patience with yourself. If you are an older person you must realize that you will not learn quickly.

Learning to drive at a late age is difficult because you are attempting to learn a skill where coordination is involved. New habits have to be formed. The element of fear enters the picture. You may need thirty or more hours of training before you reach your goal.

If you are afraid of going into heavy traffic, do not go. It is important to stay within yourself. Be satisfied with the driving you are capable of doing. Perhaps after more exposure, you will be able to cope with more complex traffic problems. If not, remember that limited driving is better than no driving at all. Do not listen to people who try to push you to drive to places where traffic is too fast or too involved. Do not necessarily drive to different places by the shortest route. Go the safest way.

You do not have to drive out of your neighborhood at the beginning. As you improve you should be able to venture further. Let your common sense be your guide. Many older people are content to be neighborhood drivers.

A limited phobic driver usually feels no qualms when driving in familiar territory. The panic is triggered when going into a different area, although the traffic conditions are similar. The solution is obvious. If the phobic person has the courage to drive into the new area often, the panic will evaporate naturally. Once the area becomes familiar, the panic will subside–trust me!

Many people have an irrational fear of driving when they try to drive away from their immediate neighborhood. They only feel comfortable in familiar surroundings. Fear of getting lost might also cause anxiety. When this happens, all you have to do is drive into the first service station you see. The attendants are usually very willing to help you. Getting lost could be a helpful experience. You will feel better about yourself after you find your way. When starting out, be sure your car has a full tank of gasoline.

"Nothing ventured, nothing gained" may be an often used cliche, but it is very meaningful to a phobic driver. How important is it for you to be able to drive anywhere you have to go? Make up your mind that you will conquer this frustrating obsession. Recognize the fact that you know how to drive. If you can drive in your neighborhood, you should be able to drive anywhere. High bridges and multi-lane highways are paved just as they are in your area. The traffic rules are the same. The lanes on bridges and multi-lane highways are usually well defined.

At first, try to drive to these places when the traffic is light. Do not try it only once a month. Do it at least twice a week. A good plan is to drive a little further each time. If you get panicky, go as far as you can and go back. Try again in a day or two and go a little further. Talk to yourself and convince yourself that you can do it. Joke about your predicament. Do not be too serious. Be casual and do not brood. Do not set a time limit. This attitude will alleviate any pressure you may feel. Do not procrastinate. Every time you drive a little further, your subconscious will record it. There are institutions which treat people with driving phobias. Their concept and cure is to get you behind the wheel, which is what this book strongly advocates.

Many drivers in their eighties have failing eyesight or deteriorating motor skill. To be sure, see an ophthalmologist and your regular medical doctor. If you are told not to drive, you must heed their advice and the advice of your relatives.

If after reading this book, you still do not have the courage to try, think about this. You are only on this earth once. After this life is finished, what lies ahead is questionable. Do not let time pass you by. You are alive now. Everyone who aspires to drive should try. Make the most of it. Do not be a bystander. Do it now.

You can not overcome your fear of driving or fear of anything by listening to tapes. Americans spend more than fifty million dollars annually on subliminal tapes. Research at the University of Northern Colorado, showed that people who listened to these tapes were not helped.

There is only one way to conquer your fear. You must realize this unalterable fact. You must attempt to do the very thing you fear.

THINKING AND WISHING WILL NOT DO IT. MAKE UP YOUR MIND THAT YOU WILL GET BEHIND THE STEERING WHEEL AND DRIVE.

There is no definitive reason for a driving phobia. Sometimes parents can implant fear of driving into their children. Some people become phobic after being involved in auto crashes. This can also be triggered by the prospect of driving over a high bridge, through a long tunnel or into heavy traffic. Phobic drivers may suffer from sweaty palms, a dry mouth, a pounding heart or a general feeling of uneasiness and trepidation. Driving phobia can manifest itself in some people after years of driving. Some phobic drivers have other fears, but many of them only have a fear of driving. It is possible that a self assured person could have an irrational fear of driving.

If driving a car is an integral part of your life, do not surrender to your fear. I have helped many phobic drivers to conquer their fear by encouraging them and helping them to drive successfully.

There are phobia treatment centers you can contact for help. They advocate the same treatment. Get behind the wheel and drive! According to a spokesman for the Anxiety Disorders Associates of America, eighty to ninety percent of these driving phobics will be able to drive again. The ten or twenty percent who cannot conquer their fear of driving are not motivated enough.

Suppose you could drive a certain way in which your chances of being involved in an accident would be infinitesimal. There is such a way. You <u>must always drive with patience</u>. That is the number one rule. Stay in your lane, preferably on your right. Be alert so you will observe all traffic regulations. Do not exceed the speed limit. If you stay in the right lane, you can drive slightly below the maximum speed limit. Do not crowd the vehicle in front of you. Stay in your lane by looking straight ahead. Do not let yourself get distracted by anything in or outside of your car. Be sure to check the rear (quickly) by glancing in the rear mirror every ten or twenty seconds. Try not to use the brake unnecessarily. Most of the time you just have to touch it gently.

By adhering to the foregoing rules, you should have an accident free record. Of course, there is no guarantee that an intoxicated driver will not strike your vehicle. There is no guarantee that the meat you buy or the fish you eat is not tainted. There is a risk involved just getting out of bed and going out into the world. Nothing is sure. Driving the way I have described, almost puts a safety net around you. There are millions of people who drive safely for thirty or forty years. It can be done.

If no one ever drove over the speed limit, and if no one ever drove under the influence, traffic fatalities could be cut in half. There is no way to stop certain people from speeding. These drivers are always in a hurry. Whether they are late for an appointment or not, they must go to the front of the pack. If the speed limit is forty-five, they drive fifty-five or sixty. This madness is prevalent in every civilized country.

My experience with thousands of frightened drivers has proven that those who persevered eventually overcame their fear. If you tried to drive before, try again. I promise you that your fear and anxiety will diminish. You have nothing to lose and everything to gain, including your independence, freedom and peace of mind. Just do it and be happy.

Everyone depicted in this book was just as frightened as you. They had the courage to try. Do not believe that you are more frightened or more nervous than anyone else. All you need is the motivation, desire and tenacity.

Good luck and safe driving.

THE END

ABOUT THE AUTHOR

Norman Klein has over 36 years of experience in driver training. He has helped countless numbers of people overcome their fear of driving to become safe, capable and independent drivers. In October, 1989, the Philadelphia Inquirer featured Mr. Klein in a special section about the driving problems of older people. The several women interviewed credited him with restoring their confidence and ultimately, their ability to drive.

In 1968, the Pennsylvania Department of Public Instruction approved a correspondence course for professional driving instructors written by Mr. Norman Klein.

Mr. Klein has personally taught approximately five thousand people, of all ages, to drive. In 1985, he successfully completed a course in Driver Training given by the Pennsylvania State University Institute of Public Safety.

Drive Without Fear is the result of over 36 years of experience teaching people to drive. This book describes stories of 20 people who overcame their fear driving due to the expertise of Mr. Klein. *Drive Without Fear* also provides a wealth of driving safety tips from which all drivers can benefit.

Mr. Klein has been married for over 40 years and has two sons, one of whom is a doctor, the other a lawyer.

Printed in the United States
141867LV00002B/1/A

9 781587 215001